CHEATINGLAND

CHEATINGLAND

THE SECRET
CONFESSIONS
OF MEN
WHO STRAY

ANONYMOUS

ATRIA BOOKS

New York • London • Toronto • Sydney • New Delhi

An Imprint of Simon & Schuster, Inc.
1230 Avenue of the Americas
New York, NY 10020

Copyright © 2022 by Anonymous

First Atria Books hardcover edition March 2022

ATRIA BOOKS and colophon are trademarks of Simon & Schuster, Inc.

For information about special discounts for bulk purchases, please contact Simon & Schuster Special Sales at 1-866-506-1949 or business@simonandschuster.com.

The Simon & Schuster Speakers Bureau can bring authors to your live event. For more information or to book an event, contact the Simon & Schuster Speakers Bureau at 1-866-248-3049 or visit our website at www.simonspeakers.com.

Interior design by Dana Sloan

Manufactured in the United States of America

1 3 5 7 9 10 8 6 4 2

Library of Congress Cataloging-in-Publication Data

ISBN 978-1-4767-0578-1
ISBN 978-1-4767-0584-2 (ebook)

CONTENTS

CONTENTS

CHAPTER ONE

INTO CHEATINGLAND

I was sitting in the locker room after a workout, talking about nothing with the guys, when someone I'll call Adam kicked opened the door to another world. He looked around the room to make sure no one would overhear him and then—in a tone you'd use to tell your friends about a bank heist you'd just pulled off—he said, "I got a new girl." His spine straightened as if a pulse of electricity had zipped through it.

"We were in the Hilton yesterday. She is crazy! The sex is *insane!*" He said things had been building for a while. "We've been flirting for years, okay, and nothing ever happened until one day it just . . . happened. We know it's wrong. But the sex is ridiculous because it's grimy." This guy knew he was playing with fire, and he liked that. Breathlessly, he went into detail about their wildest sexcapade. Meanwhile, Adam's wife was sitting outside, waiting to drive him home.

"The other day my girlfriend parked her car down the street from my house and waited for my wife to leave to go to work." We were hanging on his every word. "As soon as she saw her drive away, she pulled in. My heart was beating so fast it was crazy." After Adam finished his story, everyone walked out of the locker room, said hi to his wife, and gave her hugs, as if nothing unusual had been said.

A month later, another friend invited me out to dinner, saying that he had something he wanted to show me. I arrived at the restaurant to find that he had booked a table for three. Then he strolled in beaming with pride because he had a woman on his arm. I had dinner with him and his girlfriend of three months while our wives were at our sons' evening martial arts class. His girlfriend was also married. They weren't even considering breaking up their respective homes, but they enjoyed each other and loved the thrill of their clandestine relationship and their intense sex. The action took place in an apartment they'd slip off to after work, a place she referred to as "Cheatingland." She made it sound like Cheatingland was a clandestine little country with its own customs—sort of Fantasy Island, where wedding vows were forgotten and normally mild-mannered people could morph into sexual beasts.

After those two encounters, I started thinking about how

many men I knew who had cheated on their wives. I thought back to all the men who had whispered or crowed about what they'd done and all the men I'd heard about who were running around in the shadows with women they weren't married to. I realized that there are a lot of men ducking in and out of Cheatingland. It seemed to be pretty common even though it was an extremely dangerous place to visit. The risk of ruining one's marriage, if not one's life, was really high—I knew people who'd been caught cheating, and it destroyed their families—so what were the cheaters really looking for that was worth the risk? If it was just about sex, you could hire a prostitute, but these men were not doing that; they were chasing and sleeping with women who weren't professionals. How did they keep from getting caught? And what happened when they did get caught? I began wondering what sort of man would do that. Is there a type of man? Are there certain traits that link men who cheat?

I thought about the ones I knew. They seemed like a unique breed, many of them egotistical, brash, bold, thrill seeking, and hypersexual, with lots of what millennials call Big Dick Energy. But there were significant differences within the group. Some guys had been crazy when they were single and kept it up when they were married. Some guys seemed like they were trying to make up for lost time after having been not all that successful with women before they were married. Some were in unhappy unions, but plenty of them lived in happy homes. I knew men who loved their wives immensely but were nonetheless willing to leap into bed with someone else and saw no contradiction in that. There's a Russian roulette aspect to all of it: some men get away with it for years, while others get caught and ruin their lives. Most husbands don't cheat on their spouses, but lots do, and a lot more men get away with it than wives realize.

But what's the real reason why men cheat? Is it really about the pursuit of sex or the thrill of the hunt, or is there something missing from their marriage that they are trying to find elsewhere? Or is it some void within themselves? Is sex enough, or do they need a relationship, too? Are they getting revenge on their spouses? Have their wives done something wrong, or are some men simply socialized to be unfaithful despite that wedding band on their finger? Are they trying to prove something to themselves? Searching for a new partner? Do they just want to have more than one woman? Or was there some emotional need they were trying to fulfill? The more I thought about the men I knew, the more I realized I knew almost nothing about this behavior that so many of them were engaging in.

As a society, it seems like we can't stop talking about cheating. It's a theme in countless movies, TV shows, songs, and novels. Forbidden sex is steamy, seedy, titillating cultural catnip. And it's not just in the culture: go to any cocktail party, have a few drinks, and get deep into a one-on-one with someone who feels like he can trust you, and odds are he's got a cheating story to tell, either about a friend, or about their spouse, or about themselves. Most people think cheating is wrong, yet a lot of folks are doing it.

Having an affair fills every day with danger: one wrong move, one wrong word, and a cheater's life might explodes. No one wants to hurt his spouse. No one wants to lose his kids. No one wants to be the reason why his family fell apart. And yet people keep flocking to Cheatingland partly because the combination of lust and risk plugs a relationship into a high-voltage electric outlet. The person you're not supposed to talk to, not supposed to be alone with, not supposed to be having sex with? That person can be insanely alluring precisely because she's off-limits. Many people dismiss men who cheat as dogs and women who cheat as whores, but there must be more behind the choice to cheat than a simple lack of character or an animalistic desire for sex.

As my friends' stories about cheating swirled around in my mind, I wondered if it was possible to get guys to talk to me in depth about what they'd done. At least ten married men I knew had confided that they'd cheated at some point, but this was mostly bragging. Could I get them to go deeper, to go beyond chest-beating stories about hotel conquests and get into honest explorations of their souls and the reasons why they had left home to play? I was a little nervous even to ask—I wanted guys to drop the façade, the bluster, the ego, and tell me things they probably hadn't told anyone, admit to a serious relationship crime, and explain their actions and motives in detail. Adultery is not against the law, but admitting to it would be more dangerous than copping to many illegal activities. It's one thing to whisper to a guy that you're banging a chick behind your wife's back. It's quite another to tell a researcher who's recording your voice that you've slept around during your marriage. But I was compelled to know why they had risked so much and what were their deeper whys.

First, I called a few friends who had, in the past, boasted to me about things they'd done. Some were willing to talk further; some were not. I noticed quickly that asking a friend to talk about this topic when he wasn't ready could mean losing the friendship entirely. Some said, "I told you that to get it off my chest; I didn't tell you that for you to remember it and bring it up later." Next, I began reaching out to friends of friends—people I didn't really know. That 1 degree of separation provided them some feeling of security, but having a friend in common also provided some trust.

The more men I found and spoke to, the more intrigued I became. Guys told me crazy stories, but they also told me about their motivations, their ways of justifying cheating, their ways of hiding it, and what their ideas about masculinity had to do with all of it. What started out as a personal curiosity and a handful of conversations suddenly became a more rigorous investigation: I would call as many men as I could and ask them similar questions. Then I would try to steer them into talking about their hows and their whys.

When men talk to their friends, they keep up their guard. It's not a time to be vulnerable, but to show how cool and untouchable they are. Men will talk to their friends about their mistresses in ways that make them sound like sexual swash-bucklers, without ever approaching the internal void or the existential pain that sent them out seeking a secret partner in the first place. Men's default position is to avoid diving into their emotions. So I had to probe while at the same time creating a safe space for them to share. I had to make them feel heard and unjudged and get them to trust that even though I would be telling their secrets, I would never betray their identities. They wanted to talk about the madcap things that happened in pursuit of extra women—I listened even though there's not much to gain there in terms of insight about the cheater's psyche, but sometimes you have to let men tell you their favorite stories and go on a bit about how great they are before they can shift into the self-analysis I needed. So, my interviews took time. Most men weren't going to talk deeply about themselves without my creating the right conditions first.

After I interviewed some friends of friends, they introduced me to a few more men who'd cheated—everyone knows at least one guy, it seems—and the list grew. I viewed this as a project for exploring the thoughts, feelings, and behavior of men who step out on their wives. I would function as a sort of anthropologist reporting from inside the wildest corner of the proverbial male locker room. I wanted to peer inside the minds and souls of these men without condemning them because, for one thing, that's too easy, and, for another, if I did, they wouldn't open up to me.

I wanted to know if they were in love with their wives. I wanted to see if they were disappointed by the institution of marriage itself, with its claims of true love being the answer to life's problems. I wanted to gauge the impact of the toxic expectations of masculinity: the boys-will-be-boys culture that views women as yet more toys to be acquired. I wanted to know if they see manhood as something that must be proven endlessly through repeated feats of masculinity, strength, sexuality, adventure, risk taking, power. Was it that guys were bored with their lives? Were they desperate for a break from adulthood? Did they want to return to a younger version of themselves? Was it their wives' fault? Could a wife do anything to stop her husband from straying? I asked questions, and more, of men who'd cheated. Their answers surprised me.

Society doesn't incentivize men to talk about their feelings. But I believe that I was able to get those I interviewed to open up and share their feelings and their stories and get down to the roots of how they feel about cheating. I undertook to change all names and many identifying details, and ultimately decided that I should be anonymous as well. While I have made many changes in details, I believe that I have preserved the essential reality of my informants. Importantly, I am presenting not portraits of specific individuals but the exploration of a landscape, an MRI of the cheating heart in general, in order to give you a better understanding of the phenomenon.

As we talked, the men seemed to open up about their experiences and feelings. Many times we got down to their most honest whys. They talked about themselves, their wives, their past girlfriends, their mothers, their fathers, their insecurities, their vulnerabilities, their anxieties, their doubts, their fears. They revealed more of themselves than they ever had before—even to their wives.

A lot of men remarked on what they felt was an unusually personal conversation. "This is like a therapy session," one said. Another said, "I feel like I'm in a psychiatrist's chair." Another: "I owe you two hundred dollars an hour." Many thanked me for the chance to talk about themselves in an unvarnished way that let them pour out their truths and explore themselves. At least one person said our conversation changed his life—after we hung up, he was overcome with the feeling that he should confess to his wife. (And he did. But we'll get to his story later.) Man after man said he'd never had a chance to open up about this topic, and many seemed relieved to be able to finally explain themselves. Many said they had admitted more to me than they had ever admitted to themselves.

* * *

As I moved through my first thirty to forty interviews, I resolved to talk only to men, because I envisioned this as a study of male behavior. But as my research progressed, I realized that I could probably learn more by also speaking to women who committed adultery. They could help me better understand men who cheat because their thoughts and experiences would add valuable context, allowing me to see how women's experiences regarding infidelity were similar to men's and how they were different. So, I began to search out and find women, both straight and lesbian, who had fascinating stories. They would become critical voices within this study. Frankly, the women were more forthcoming as well as more insightful. Most of the women I spoke to found it much easier to access their feelings—their whys. Women revealed that for them, cheating is far easier to pull off than men would ever imagine, and, sometimes, it plays an important part of self-discovery. Much more about that later.

Some of the most powerful contributors to my study were lesbians, but gay men were a different story. Even though I wanted to include them, it proved tricky. I made an effort to find those voices, and, yes, there are a small number of gay men among my subjects, but most of the gay men I spoke to admitted they slept around but also said they viewed monogamy as elastic. Neither they nor their partners regarded such behavior as cheating. I was told that for many gay couples, it's not unusual to accept partners having sex outside their relationship as long as certain ground rules are followed. The rules differ for each couple, but examples include "Don't fall in love," "Never have unprotected sex," "No sleeping with anyone the other man knows," and "Be home by two in the morning."

This was extramarital sex, but not cheating as per my definition, for cheating requires secrecy. It's not condoned within the relationship; otherwise it's an open relationship. I didn't interview people who said they were in open relationships—that's an entirely different entity. Open relationships are a fascinating reshaping of the traditional boundaries of marriage, but I wanted to explore something else. I wasn't interested in talking about extramarital affairs that were partner approved. I wanted to know about affairs where everything was at stake.

It was painstaking work to find more and more people who would talk, but over a four-year period, I interviewed sixty-one men and twelve women, each for at least an hour. I also spoke to numerous psychologists, sociologists, and sexologists for their insights and context. In the end, less than one-sixth of my subjects were people I knew before I began the study. Most of my interviews were conducted over the phone. I asked each to give me his first name only, as well as the city or region he lived in, his age, race, and general area of employment.

I collected this information to make sure I had a broad cross section of people from a variety of regions, races, and social classes. My volunteers are a diverse group: white, Black, Hispanic, and Middle Eastern. They range in age from the early twenties to the midsixties, with most falling between thirty and fifty years old. They include real estate developers, sales reps, truckers, teachers, body shop managers, stand-up

comics, attorneys, nurses, software consultants, restaura-
teurs, and more. They're from Atlanta, Baltimore, Boston,
Detroit, Houston, Indianapolis, Las Vegas, Los Angeles, New
York, San Antonio, and beyond. Some had one long affair,
some had several short affairs, some are currently in affairs,
and some got caught or quit the cheating life on their own.

I could not find many of my interview subjects again
even if I wanted to. For many, anonymity was important to
giving them the freedom to be brutally honest. I asked them
if they had cheated, how many people they had been with,
why they had done it, who had influenced them, how they
pulled it off and what they did to get away with it, whether
they had been caught and what they'd done after getting
found out, whether it was all worth it, if they felt guilty, and
much, much more. Everyone wants to tell his or her secrets;
you just need to give people the space to do it safely, including that they wouldn't feel judged.

As I worked through my research, several subjects pushed
me to reshape my definition of cheating in one critical way.
When I began my study, I defined adultery as having sex that
was kept a secret from your spouse. I wanted to talk to people
who needed it so badly that they snuck out the proverbial
back door, broke their vows, risked divorce, and then returned
home. But as I met more and more women who had cheated,
many of them said they were involved in clandestine affairs
that felt wrong morally—but these relationships were not
sexual or physical in any way. Sometimes they called these

"emotional affairs." It's telling that very few men acknowledged being involved in this kind of extramarital relationship.

At first, I wasn't going to include these stories because I
was stuck in the perspective that cheating required a physical
component. But as I listened to story after story of emotional
affairs—deep, secret connections with someone outside your
marriage, where there are feelings, flirting, and the intensity of a furtive relationship even though there's no sex—I
realized that quite often there is no substantive difference
between emotional affairs and consummated ones. People,
especially women, who engage in emotional affairs regard
them as a marital violation and refer to them as cheating.
They are taking the same risks, experiencing the same sense
of danger, and getting most of the same returns as people in
sexual affairs: the thrill of being in an illicit situation, the
psychological exhaustion from pursuing the relationship
while keeping their spouse in the dark, and the accompany-
ing guilt that induces.

After hearing many stories of emotional affairs, I realized I had to redefine *cheating* to decenter sex and instead see
it as a secret relationship that is not necessarily sexual yet is
still sexually charged. You don't have to sleep with someone
to be cheating. You can devastate your partner even without
touching someone else. For many people whose husband was
unfaithful, finding out that he was in an emotional affair can
be even more painful because it's not just meaningless sex,
it's a genuine connection. One woman said to me, "I've been

cheated on, and I've forgiven a partner for cheating on me. If it was purely physical, I'm, like, 'Okay, I'm not going to forget this, don't make a fool out of me, but I can move past that.' But emotional infidelity is a lot worse. You're sharing really heavy romantic words and ideas, and it has elements of love and romance. That right there, oh, man, that there can crush you."

*   *   *

It's easy to pass judgement on a two-timer. He's violating his vow to the most central person in his life. He's risking hurting his spouse immensely. He's jeopardizing the future of their family. And for what? Selfish pleasure? Isn't adulthood supposed to be about sublimating the imperative to constantly please yourself and instead act as if you're part of something bigger than you? Aren't you supposed to put what's best for your spouse and your children ahead of your own needs? The desire to condemn cheaters is understandable because adultery isn't a victimless crime. People have lost the unit that shaped their childhood or their adulthood because of an affair, and that can have a devastating impact. Some men have used affairs to demean or control women.

But in order to find out why people stray, I had to put aside judgement. One man who had a string of girlfriends while his wife was at home with their three kids asked me, "Do I sound like a monster?" I told him, "No, you sound like you." Admittedly, he *did* sound monstrous for fooling around while she was drowning in responsibility and diapers, but

I had to give him the freedom to answer my questions the honest way he wanted, no matter how ugly it was, because without that, I couldn't uncover his true self and his real reasons for cheating. Once we established that, we could get down to ideas that might help people understand better why and how cheaters cheat.

I'm not saying that we all need to learn to accept cheating. Every situation is different, and every person will respond in his or her own way. Some people will uncover an affair and flee the marriage. Others, despite their hurt, will find a way to reshape the relationship and forgive. Either way, I hope this book can help people think through and comprehend the real reasons why a cheater makes certain choices and what to do with that knowledge.

Many couples survive the revelation of an affair. I will talk about how they did that and what cheaters need to do to save their marriages. For now, just know that I was able to get people to tell me truths that they're not willing or able to tell their partners, so if you're trying to understand infidelity in your own life, hopefully you can use this book to bridge the gap between what someone is able to communicate and what the rest of the truth may be. This book can help you see the underlying feelings cheaters have had, so that you can understand what it was that led them astray. Whether you choose to end things or move forward as a couple is up to you, but with more perspective, you may approach your decision with greater clarity.

• • •

How many Americans are cheating? It's hard to really know because a lot of people get away with a lot of cheating. In fact, it's possible that most infidelity is never discovered. Many men told me they never got caught. The old adage that the wife always knows is definitely not true. And women find it even easier to evade detection. But large surveys conducted over the last few decades have concluded that, in the United States, about 20 percent to 25 percent of men have cheated on their wives, while approximately 15 percent to 20 percent of women have cheated on their husbands. Several researchers have found that in about half of all marriages, one partner will cheat at some point, and in roughly one in five marriages, one partner is cheating right now. According to some recent studies, increasing numbers of married women are cheating, and if you include emotional affairs, some researchers say women today are seeking intimacy outside of their marriage about as much as men.

Modern technology only makes it easier to commit adultery by connecting strangers through social media sites such as Instagram and Facebook or websites created specifically to facilitate affairs, including Ashley Madison and AdultFriend-Finder. There are more ways to meet someone who's not in your everyday social network than ever before, and that expands the number of opportunities for cheating infinitely.

Cheatingland is like a grown-up's amusement park where

you can get lost on the erotic rides, find an ego boost, indulge in unapologetic debauchery, forget about the outside world, and step outside your real life for a little while. In contrast, Marriageland, on the other hand, is like the parking lot outside the circus. It's mundane, like feeling tired from the long day and having to struggle to find your car amidst a sea of other vehicles in the train station parking lot. It's tedious, like navigating through bumper-to-bumper traffic to get to the freeway. But it's also joyous, as when everyone is laughing and singing songs together at the top of their lungs on the drive home, creating bonding moments that will stay with all of you forever. For most of us, Marriageland is what makes life worth living. It provides the stability, the balance, and the support that help you get through the days, it carries you through the tough times, it helps bring fun to the smallest moments. But despite the immense danger of losing your place in Marriageland, some people still find themselves lured toward Cheatingland. This book will help you understand why.

The next chapter looks at how husbands can cheat while still loving their wives and examines some of the core influences behind cheating. Chapter 3 unveils the five major categories of affairs and weighs the differences between them. Chapter 4 dives into the women of my study and their perspectives. Chapter 5 explores the typical cheater personality. Chapter 6 is about the many tricks and tactics that unfaithful spouses use to get away with it. Chapter 7 shines a light on the dark side of cheating—what happens when things go horribly wrong. Chapter 8 examines the reasons why some men quit cheating. And chapter 9 goes into what options cheaters have if they get caught.

In my talks with male adulterers, I heard a lot of things that men would never tell their wives. Chris from Chicago said at the end of our interview: "I guess women would be very frightened if they heard the conversation we just had. My wife would probably faint and have a heart attack if she heard, but the thing she wouldn't understand is what's really in my heart."

This book is here to tell you what that is.

CHAPTER TWO

IT'S NOT HIS WIFE'S FAULT
HE'S CHEATING

After wives find out their husbands are cheating on them, some look in the mirror and ask themselves what they could have done differently. A thirty-ish woman named Jill said that when she discovered her spouse was having an affair, she immediately blamed herself.

"I turned my anger inward," she said. "I said that if my husband cheated on me, that means I am a failure as a wife. I thought, *This is happening because I'm not doing certain things good enough*. I thought it was a symptom of me doing something wrong rather than him having a problem or both of us needing to make adjustments in our marriage. I thought I should seek counseling or just accept that my expectations of this person are unrealistic, and I need to adjust my expectations and not let this eat me alive.

"I was certain that there was something wrong with me as a wife and that, if I cleaned the house better, cooked dinner better, our marriage would be better. I was a stay-at-home mom during that time, and I thought that if I fulfilled that role better, then I could 'fix' him and make him happy and fix the marriage. I thought I should have never yelled about this or that or all this stuff. I should have been able to know what he was feeling and what he needed even when he wasn't telling me."

Like Jill, many women blame themselves for their husband's cheating. But a wide cross section of the men I interviewed made it a point to emphasize that their betrayals were not their wives' fault. Most said it wasn't a response to their wives at all. It was about the men themselves.

Many men who cheat said they're happy at home. In fact, almost all of the participants I spoke to professed to be in love with their wives and had no desire to leave or hurt them. Peter, from Denver, said, "When I was with other women, I still loved my wife. She's a bedrock part of my life. She's my heart, she's my center. I feel warm when I lay eyes on her. I see her in the morning lying beside me, and I think she's so beautiful, she's so lovely. We have a nice relationship, which, you know, isn't perfect—there's bumps in our road—but I'll take it. No relationship is perfect, but I want to be married to her forever. But I also enjoy being with other women. It makes me feel macho and badass and powerful. It's not about turning away from my wife, it's a way of pumping myself up."

Men usually don't love their affair partners, they love *having an affair*: the rush, the drama, the ego boost, the stolen moments, the sense of getting away with something, the supercharged sex. They want many things, but they don't want to hurt or reject their wives. For many men, the impulse to cheat comes from some motivation buried inside of them, which means that, in most cases, a husband's cheating cannot be blamed on his wife.

It may seem strange that men can deceive their wives and yet still love them, but that's exactly how many men see it. Women may ask, How can a man lie to his wife, betray her, sneak around behind her back, put his marriage at risk, and also love her? Is that how a loving partner behaves? But in many a cheater's mind, fooling around with someone else is not a rejection of his wife, it's a desire to add another element to his life. We see that in how philanderers tend to look for different qualities from each relationship. At home in Marriageland, they long for love and stability, but in the funhouse of Cheatingland, they're hunting for adrenaline, excitement, attention, and danger.

"All of my affairs were fairly emotionless," admitted Jeff from Portland. "I could put each part of my life in a box in my mind and not have them overlap. *This* person is for love, and *this* person is for sex, and there's no confusion over who is who." But what many men want is to have two women in their lives with whom they have distinctly different relationships. Each one serves a separate purpose. Men want a wife who helps build a happy, close-knit family, who helps him to be seen in his community as someone who has a loving unit that is a valued part of their community, thus making him look good. She helps him forge his legacy. When men cheat, they want to have another woman in their lives who pumps up their ego, helping them feel attractive, sexy, and powerful man. They want to be both the proud patriarch with an unforgettable lady at their side and the sexual animal they felt like when they were younger. These are two distinct areas that cannot be inhabited easily by the same woman.

Men know that Cheatingland is a place you go to get away, unwind, and have a totally different experience than in your normal life. But it's value and power come from being temporary. Plus, Cheatingland is fun because the risk is high (he's full of adrenaline because he's doing something that our culture generally regards as wrong), but the emotional investment is low (his affair partner can't really hurt his feelings). Most of the male subjects I interviewed said they were not invested emotionally in their affair, so it wasn't the end of the world if they got dumped in Cheatingland. Not like, say, losing your spouse and possibly your kids, too.

Cheatingland is a space where both parties in an affair are presenting the best versions of themselves to each other.

Randy, a married fortysomething in Maryland who's in a long-term side relationship, said, "It's an idealized situation. She's always perfumed. She's always wearing sexy underwear. She's always got energy for sex, and she's always open to it. She's always attentive to my needs. You're not cutting a fart in front of each other. It's an oasis." People get to see an idealized slice of their affair partner's personality, as opposed to being present for their spouse's every mood. Cheaters generally don't have to deal with their partner's flaws, they don't get turned down sexually, they usually don't get into the fights that are a common part of living together for decades. In Cheatingland, there are no real responsibilities and no baggage. It's an escape from your life.

Molly said, "In an affair, you don't get the warts and the perspective that you have when you're in a relationship that has ups and downs and good days and bad days and the stressors of families and real-life obligations. In the affair, you're in a bubble. And in a bubble, little else exists. It works for us, but we're not fooled by the fact that it's not reality. That's part of what makes it work."

In Marriageland, however, people's flaws are on full display; they're part of the package. Men and women vow to love each for better or worse, for richer or poorer, in sickness and in health, and marriage will be full of these and other ups and downs. In Marriageland, people see each other at their best and their worst. They see each other happy and frazzled and angry and silly and every other emotion on the spectrum.

Two partners may share the uplifting joys and crushing pains of raising children and the roller coaster of being an adult. All of this can make it a struggle to keep a relationship fresh and fun and to keep your sex life going. Those challenges can help bond a couple. Randy, the married fortysomething from Maryland, who said he loves sleeping around but is resolute about not leaving his wife, put it this way:

"My girlfriend and I had a utopian relationship where there wasn't the day-to-day bullshit. But part of the reason why I stuck with my wife is that she's seen me at my worst, and she's still with me. And I've seen her at her worst, and I still love her. It's real love when someone's seen your dirty drawers, and they still love you. It makes me feel really safe in our marriage that we don't have to maintain a fantasy for each other. She loves me as I really am, and I love her."

Still, in marriage sometimes, people can end up feeling forgotten and unseen and in need of some extra attention. Brett from Seattle, who's been cheating on his wife with several women, said, "Cheating almost felt like a way for me to take a little bit of control back in my own life. I was making a decision so far outside of anything that she would approve of or have any real say over. I think that was a big part of it. I just needed to do something *I* wanted to do, something for myself, and that is to give myself the gift of amazing, heart-pounding sex."

For many people, that is at the crux of the matter. In Cheatingland, the sex is bountiful and incendiary. Spousal sex cannot compete with cheating sex, almost every man said. Sex is one of the greatest gifts in the world, and when you make it forbidden and add a strong element of risk, you get an intoxicating rush. "It's electric," said Scott from Dallas. Adding yet another element of debauchery, Scott keeps a list of exactly how many women he's slept with because he's in competition with his friends. "You know you're not supposed to be there, you're not supposed to be with this person, but you are," he explained. "The wrongness of it all, plus the feeling of getting away with something, plus the thrill of getting something extra—all of that just adds up to an explosion."

Scott wasn't the only man to feel this way. Eddie, a thirtysomething engineer, said, "I'm an adrenaline junkie. If it's not scaring me, I'm not doing it. I'm that kind of guy that will jump off a bridge with bungee cords. And going behind closed doors with someone outside your marriage when nobody knows what you're doing, that's a huge adrenaline rush."

Ethan, from Michigan: "I think the risk is what makes it enticing; as if you're dodging a bullet all the time. The risk is what keeps the adrenaline and the passion of it going." The more wicked the sex, the more the heart races and the mind focuses and the act engulfs you. Unfaithful men said repeatedly that the sinful, immoral, transgressive nature of cheating sex gave it a turbo boost that loving sex at home can't match.

My friend Adam, whom we met at the beginning of chapter 1, is now having unbelievable sex with another woman. "We know that it's wrong," he said. "Everything about it is wrong. But I'm telling you, the sex is absurd. It's risk-your-life good, which is good because I am definitely risking my life for this. She knows my wife, I know her husband, they've both been to our house. He would kill me, and then my wife would revive me so that *she* could kill me. It's not that my wife's sex isn't good—it is—but with this girl, it's great because I'm not supposed to be doing it."

Sam, an attorney from New Orleans, has had many affairs. "There's something about breaking the rules and doing things you know you shouldn't be doing," he observed. "There's definitely a draw to that. It's a thrill-seeking adrenaline thing, like you're in an episode of *Mission: Impossible*, and you're just trying to figure out how to get to the next day." People in an illicit relationship may look at the electricity of their encounters and think they have some special connection, but in most cases, the spark comes from the secretive nature of their trysts. If, let's say, they left their respective spouses and married each other, the sex no doubt would quickly lose that zing. But as long as there's something taboo about them being together, their tie will have that charged feeling that marriage cannot match. Men love their affairs for totally different reasons than they love their marriages. Many cheaters want both because they're fundamentally different experiences.

Paul, a Texas restaurateur who's had a long string of affairs spoke of a scene from a movie where a wife went to work at strip club so she could learn new ways to turn on her husband, who had a thing for strippers. On her first night there, she asked a veteran stripper for advice. The veteran stripper said something like, "Well, the first thing honey, is you're his wife. So it's never going to work.".

"I was, like, 'Damn, that's cold!' " Paul said. "But it's real, and that's what you get from screwing around: something totally different from what you get from your wife, and that's because screwing around is what I call holiday behavior. 'Cause when you're alone with her, you're on holiday. You forget about your everyday lifestyle and just live in that moment, and there's no inhibitions and no restrictions. Because of that, me and my side girl had crazy, crazy, incredible sex. In the back of my mind, I said I would love to have this at home. But no matter how much fun the holiday was, I never, never played with the idea of this woman taking the place of my wife. That was never a thought in my mind. I did think, *I would love to have sex like this with my wife*, but you know you can't have that kinda freedom with your wife."

Rarely does the mistress eventually become the cheater's wife perhaps because of the "Madonna-whore" complex. Some men see women as either saintly or sexual, as either wives to be respected and put on a pedestal (which may mean no sex or vanilla sex), or as sex partners who are not respectable. When someone has that mindset, a mistress could never take the place of a wife. Eric, from California, married for fifteen years, said he had another woman in his life because he wanted two different relationships at once. "I do things with this woman that I've never done with my wife and that I probably don't *want* to do with my wife," he said. "I don't mean to get too explicit, but she swallows, okay? My wife doesn't. And that's okay. I don't want to kiss this girl after she swallows all that shit, you know? With my wife, I want all that passionate kissing because I love her. If we ever do have sex, I hold my wife. I make sure we cuddle because I love her. With my other woman, after we finish, I don't hold her. It's more, like, 'Okay, all right, we're done, let's sit up and get our drink on, or whatever.'"

Ethan from Michigan, said, "I love my wife. When we got married, I could not see myself marrying anyone else. She was the girl that, even though you're not ready, you just can't let this one get by—one of those type of things. So, I fell in love with her, man, and about a year later, on the road, I met a girl, and we screwed around for a couple of years. It wasn't that I wasn't getting what I wanted at home, it was just being greedy. It was just wanting that extra attention and needing the thrill of being a predator, you know what I mean? Me being a predator and women being the prey. That's where I got the excitement out of it. And my wife's a good church girl—she grew up in the church, her dad is in the ministry, and she was raised to be a certain way—but, let's just say, in the bedroom, when we were dating and fooling around, she was a bad girl. But after she became my wife, when I brought up certain things I wanted to do, it would be 'Ehhhh, that's kinda wild, that's kinda nasty,' or whatever.

"So I was a little bored until I met my other, and then I was basically getting my excitement out of her. My wife was that stability, she was that forever part of my life, but this other girl was scratching my itches, if you know what I mean. And I was kinda lying to myself saying, 'Hey, well, since my wife won't do it, it's okay.' I still had a happy relationship. When I was at home, my mind was on home, I was focused on her, I'd be in home mode. But when I was on the road, my friend would come and visit me wherever I was. I didn't think there was anything that my wife was missing from a relationship standpoint. You know, we'd have those pillow talks to make sure everything's okay, but in the back of my mind, I was like, *I need more wildness, and you're not willing to go there, so part of me can't wait to get back on the road.*

"So, you know, it got kinda crazy because we were fooling around for about seven years, and she was kinda my little side chick. She didn't mind being that at all, and we had fun together. Then I'd get back on the plane, and I'd transform into husband-man, and everything's great. People were looking at me and my wife, wanting to be like us, and looking up to us, but I couldn't be that without my little escapes from it."

Many men say that they see their wives as existing on a pedestal: she's a classy lady who's above having crazy sex.

Maybe they did those things with her when they were dating, but after marrying, she's elevated. But if he still wants to get into the gutter sometimes and engage his kinks, that's what his side chick is for: someone with whom he can indulge his wild side. This is especially the case if she's someone he sees as social inferior, with lower status than him or his wife. This is partly because America's sexual conservatism and puritan underpinnings lead many of us to feel ashamed of our more unique desires, or, at least, to feel like we should hide them. Men who want something that's far off the standard menu may feel uncomfortable asking their wife—if she says no, that's even more of a reason to feel ashamed. But if we had a greater sense of sexual freedom, a broader and more inclusive notion of what constitutes acceptable, "normal" desires, then perhaps fewer men would need to seek outsiders who are willing to play games with them that society has deemed strange.

When wives discover that their husband has a mistress, they often look down on the so-called other woman unable to imagine what he could possibly see in her. "Why is he with *her*? She's not on my level." But that's the point. A cheater doesn't leave home looking to find someone who is like his wife or someone he hopes can replace his wife. He's looking for the low-rent yin to her high-value yang. Someone with whom he can have an easy, wild, sex-filled romp as a counterbalance to the complex, mature life he's building with his wife. So if his wife is classy, then he's probably looking for something else entirely in a mistress. Even though that other personality might not be obvious at first glance.

Randy, who's in several relationships including his marriage, said, "One of my affair partners has a certain persona in her work industry, in the outside world, where she is very prim and proper. But once you get her behind closed doors, holy shit! I'll go out with her and get maybe three hours of sleep over the course of nine hours that night. It'll be a crazy, exhausting evening with people getting tied up and hanging from the ceiling, and costumes and whatever wildness you can think of. We like seeing how far we can push things. It's basically a surreal environment. We're very open about particular fantasies that we have, and we can really talk about anything, and you do go for anything you can imagine because you're getting that person for just a short period of time. We go in the room, and she's a total and absolute freak, and then she buttons up and walks out, and you'd never know that she's like that."

With a mistress in their lives, men can explore their adventurous side and push the envelope of their sexuality while keeping their weirdness out of their marriage so that their home life can stay sweet and pure. They can pursue and have great sex in Cheatingland while still wanting and valuing the love they get at home. Being part of a family makes them feel good, and being one half of a nasty, crazy affair also makes them feel good. Both sides are part of what we've been told a real man does. A real man takes care of his family. A real man also has—or seeks to have—his own harem. For men who cheat, both desires consume them simultaneously and sometimes quite harmoniously.

Millennials have popularized the acronym *YOLO*, meaning "you only live once" (so go ahead and do stupid things). You know that YOLO behavior is dumb and self-destructive, but you do it anyway. The sense that life is short and you have to grab as much happiness as you can is part of the mentality of many cheaters. Nathan, an actor from Cleveland, remarked, "I always tried to self-analyze why I was doing it. Maybe it's an excuse, but I had a lot of tragedy as a kid. Lost my dad young to suicide. Lost other members of my family, too, when I was young. It was like I was getting hit with death after death. I come from a world where there were many suicides and deaths, and I think my whole philosophy on life was shaped in, like, sixth grade.

"So I looked at life with a really crooked outlook, like I thought I wasn't going to live past twenty-five or something. I was kind of wild, and I used to just convince myself that life is short, so play hard and do whatever I want. I'm a good guy, and getting laid on the road doesn't mean anything. I don't love these girls, and I was never starting a real relationship. I never had, like, an *affair*. I would just *cheat*. So, it was my own twisted vision of life that let me say, 'Hey, it's cool for me to do this.' My life-is-short philosophy is what fueled it."

Cheating is YOLO on steroids. Men committing adultery

know they're being counterproductive; they know they're at a metaphorical casino gambling with their mortgage money; they know they're risking everything for a brief, selfish thrill. But they tell themselves that it's okay. They often tend to be gifted at justifying their behavior.

"There's an ego play in all of this," said Steve, a radio host from the Midwest. "You feel the entitlement: 'I'm such-and-such in my life, in my profession, I'm killing it at work, I do so much for my family, but I'm not getting everything I want at home, so, like, Fuck it! I deserve a little bit of joy! I am entitled to do this.' If I'm being absolutely honest, I understand that.

"I had a birthday recently," Steve told me, "and it was a particularly shitty birthday. My birthday was really an afterthought in my house. It was mentioned, but it wasn't, like, a *thing* like it really should be. And that's not the norm. My wife is usually really thoughtful when it comes to birthdays, but this year she wasn't—for whatever reason. But I deserve joy, so I slipped out to see my affair partner one day right after my birthday because I was, like, 'Fuck it, *that's* my birthday present. I want an insane afternoon of endless, sore-inducing, can't-walk-after-it sex. You know, a real wild tornado whirlwind.

"Well, I got that, and I was happy. After that, I did not care one bit about what my wife didn't do for my birthday. Wiped all my resentments away."

Men talk about extramarital sex as if it's the one thing

that can end all pain. No matter what's bothering him, any man who recently slept with his mistress is too happy to care. Many say it allows them to avoid injecting their frustration into their marriage. Kevin, who's had several affairs, said, "You know how a drug addict feels, like how all the problems in the world go away when they get that shit in their veins or in their lungs or whatever? All my worries went away as soon as my dick was inside another girl. I felt like the baddest man in the world. Crack couldn't possibly be as good as pussy you're not supposed to have.

"When I was getting that," he continued, "I had less stress in my life. I didn't worry about small things. I would definitely not fight or argue, because I was so happy. Any slight, any comment would just roll off my back because I had my secret thing going on. I know that they say, 'Happy wife, happy life,' but, look, for me to give her the happy life she needs, I've gotta have the happy life I need."

Cheating can compensate for sexual frustration, but, in reality, it's like a Band-Aid covering a wound that's still festering; the man still has issues that are bringing him pain. Many times, his sexual frustration masks something far deeper in his past. Cheating on his wife may provide some sexual comfort food to help him get through the day, but his issues can quite often be significant ones that have nothing to do with the desire for more sex.

For many men, touch is an essential love language. They need physicality to feel manly and actualized and engaged. If you remove touching, physicality, and sex, it's hard for them to really experience love. Without sex, they may feel weak, worthless, unseen. So if their marital lovemaking ends or decreases to the point where they are not getting anywhere near the amount of sex that they need—or they are not getting the intensity or the duration or the passion they need—this can lead to an internal crisis. *Am I still a man? If no woman wants me, what sort of man am I?*

Many men contend that satisfying their sexual frustration through extramarital sex enables them to feel like men again. They may cheat as part of an internal conversation: *Am I still a man? Who am I becoming? Can I still* attract *women?* Sure, they're proud of being the husband and the dad and taking care of their family, yet they still miss the stud they used to be.

Listen to Nick, from Connecticut: "I used to meet my ex-girlfriend once every few months so we could bang each other's brains out. We'd always find someplace new: maybe an upscale restaurant bathroom, or a motel, or we'd borrow a friend's apartment. We were only okay as a couple, but we were always amazing in bed, and that kept us coming back to each other. I didn't love her; I loved having wild sex with her. I felt terrible about lying to my wife, but I needed that oasis of wild sex in a sea of grocery stores, long car rides, recitals, bedtimes, meltdowns—I needed someplace where I could remember that I used to be *the man*. The chance to get that was irresistible."

Men did not say, "I'm mad at my wife, so I'm going to go have an affair." They said they cheated because they wanted to feel badass, manly, and alpha; they wanted to get back to the self-image they had when they were younger. It's the same impulse that may lead other men to start a rock band or buy a Porsche. Men who are at an uncertain place in their lives and low on self-esteem may be wondering, *What am I good at? What makes me special? What's my niche?* The answer to their questions may come in the form of sexual power; the way they're able to woo women. For many men, winning the approval of female strangers is essential to their self-image. This is partly about the looking-glass self, a sociological concept invented by Charles Horton Cooley that says the way you believe society views you deeply influences the way you view yourself. People develop their perception of themselves partly from how they are seen by others. Our social interactions tell us how others see us because we tend to see ourselves as a reflection of our connections with other people. How someone regards us—kind, wise, smart, sweet, powerful, frightening, and so on—that will be apparent from how he or she interacts with us. And that external judgement of us shapes how we see ourselves.

For men who need to be seen as successful with the opposite sex, motivating women to sleep with them means they are the person they wish to be. This is part of what infidelity expert Esther Perel says in her book *The State of Affairs: Rethinking Infidelity*: "It's not so much that you want to leave the person that you're with. It's that you want to leave the person that you've become." The Belgian-born psychotherapist sees infidelity as an exploration of the self and a search for a new identity. Many of the men I spoke to confirmed this, telling me they saw the physical space where they were cheating as practically a different world because it was a place that allowed them to become a different person. Ethan, from Michigan, said, "When you're out there with other women, you get to get away from being the guy at home that you don't like." Jamie from Atlanta said, "I was looking for excitement. I was looking for the freedom to be, like, myself, you know, even though the self I wanted to be was an immature jackass. A boy. But I just wanted to be that—and with that particular woman, I was allowed to be that."

Several men said the self-loathing that was suffocating them in Marriageland all but vanished once they ventured into Cheatingland, which shouldn't come as a surprise. After all, probably the quickest cure for seeing yourself as bland is to find a new member of the opposite sex who thinks you're hot. Seeing yourself through her eyes is so addictive that people will go through a lot just to revel in that sensation. Yes, they're after electric, forbidden sex. Yes, they're after the ego boost. But they're also wanting to transform their own vision of themselves.

In my interviews, numerous men said their cheating was a way to reclaim their youthful glory and relive the wild sexuality that they loved about their younger selves—they're bored by who they are and want to get back to who they used to be. Mark from Las Vegas said, "Inside the box of our house, I'm happy, but outside the box, I need to know that I'm accepted by other beautiful women. I need to prove it to myself again."

*   *   *

For many adulterers, infidelity is deeply connected to what it means to be a man, which makes sense because many men first learned about manhood from their fathers—with many first learning from them, either directly or through example, that cheating on one's wife is part and parcel of being a man. In my study, the most common element linking cheaters, the element that most of them shared, is knowing that their dad had cheated on their mom or that Dad had openly encouraged them to cheat. Some fathers set an example without ever saying a word about sex or women—some cheaters said they knew Dad was sneaking around because they saw him doing it.

One man told me that when he got to high school, a family elder pulled him aside and cautioned, "You are free to date anyone in school except ——. She might be your sister." But many cheaters said their fathers openly encouraged them to fool around. Brett said, "A day before I got married, my dad said to me, in a kind of mocking tone, 'Get ready for the last piece of ass you'll ever have!' Here I was all excited about getting married, and, in a second, he kind of turned me around.

I was, like, 'I never thought of it like that, but that's cool. I ain't backing out. I love her.'

"But that sarcastic comment stuck in my head, and, days later, it led to a discussion where my dad and my uncle were both telling me, 'Listen, man, enjoy your woman as long as you can. That's cool. But there may come a time where you want to step out and explore. That's cool too. Just be responsible. Just don't fuck things up with your woman. Be responsible. Strap up and go back home without falling in love.' I thought, *I ain't planning on cheating; that's not what I want to do. I ain't y'all. I'm in love, and I'm marrying her because I want a family.*

"Well, we started our marriage on the right foot. I was totally committed to her. But in time, Dad's voice kept coming back to me: '*Last piece* of ass *you'll ever have*' ... 'There may come a time where you want to step out and explore. That's cool too.' And years after we got married, I took heed." You could say that Brett's father indoctrinated him. After all, the son entered marriage not thinking about sleeping around. But his dad planted the idea in his mind and, more importantly, gave him permission.

Sam, from New Orleans, learned more by example. "My dad was a big-time womanizer in his day," he said. "He was a singer—even had a recording contract—who grew up in that whole Rat Pack, big band era, and he would tell stories about sleeping with every waitress at a club. Now, I knew that my mom was at home with us at the time when he was out doing that, so that probably skewed my behavior to an extent."

Most of the men who cheated were influenced by their father and this is consistent with studies that have found that children who were aware of a parent's infidelity are more likely to have sex outside of marriage when they become adults. According to clinical psychologist Ana Nogales, author of *Parents Who Cheat: How Children and Adults Are Affected When Their Parents Are Unfaithful*, 55 percent of children who have an unfaithful parent grow up to be cheaters. This pattern played out in my study too, even among men who said their dad's infidelity traumatized them.

Kevin said, "I remember seeing my dad cheat on my mom when I was, like, five. I've never told anyone this story. My mom and dad were married, and we were at his girlfriend's house. I walked in the bedroom and saw him and his girlfriend having sex, and he told me to get out. I was hungry, so I went to the refrigerator, and there was nothing in there except cheese. Standard, plastic-wrapped cheese.

"Later on, I did something with my cousin that wasn't appropriate, I laid on top of her, but I thought I was doing what dad had done with his girlfriend. I've never told anybody this. Mom came in and caught me and flipped out. She said, 'What are you doing?' I said, 'I saw Dad doing that on top of this woman.' Then Mom really lost it. Next thing you know, they're in the kitchen fighting, and she's yelling, 'How could you do this?' She beat him up, and that was the last time I saw my father. They got a divorce, and I haven't seen him since that day. I think that moment seriously screwed me up. Seeing him like that and having our family explode like that really, really messed me up sexually."

Ironically, this boy who witnessed an affair and saw it destroy his family still grew up to be a cheater himself. "I don't know why," Kevin said, "but seeing him do it means I have to do it." Dad sets the son's example of what a man is, and if that includes sleeping around, then the boy may grow up to associate that with "manly" behavior—even if he knows firsthand from a young age that the consequences can be devastating.

Some men said Dad did more than just give them license: he taught them how to do it. "I used to sit in my dad's office, and he'd be sitting on the phone straight pimpin,'" said Jackson, a thirtysomething Los Angeleno. "I loved watching him pimpin'. He wasn't married to my mom then—he was remarried—but he was still chasing women like he was single, and I'd be sitting there listening to his rap. That rap became my rap. I learned to chase women from him."

Nathan, the actor from Cleveland, recalled, "When I was dating my girl in college—my first real, real serious girl—my dad did say something to me one time that stuck with me. He said, 'No matter what goes down, don't admit it.' That's my hero telling me if I cheat, don't admit anything ever. I never knew him to cheat on my mom—I never heard about it, never seen it—but he encouraged *me* to do it, and I took that to heart. That had a heavy impression on me. If my hero was going to say that, then I'd do it."

Many men who didn't know their fathers or weren't close to them said they received the green light to cheat from other older men in their families. For example, Sam was influenced by an uncle. "I thought he was like the cool uncle," he remembered, "but he was way younger than my mom, so he was probably only twenty years older than me. He was always pointing out all the hot girls in the crowd. If we were in a grocery store, he'd be grabbing me and showing me a girl with a nice ass. He'd say, 'I want to have her sit on my face!' This when I was *six years old*! I'd be, like, "Yeah, that's weird. Why would she sit on your face?' I didn't even know what the hell he was talking about. But he seemed very hypersexual and studly and cool, so I thought that's how a man is supposed to be.

"In reality," Sam added, "he was living at his mother's house. In retrospect, he was kind of a loser. But when I was eight, I thought he was awesome and that I should be like him."

For Scott from Dallas, permission to fool around came from his grandfather. "There was once a conversation with my grandpa," he remembered, "where he said something I never expected to hear from him. He made the comment "Always have backup." It made me laugh because he was joking, but he was also dead serious."

Chris from Chicago said, "My grandfather was the first

person to show me how to be a player. He told me that *he* was a player. He wasn't hiding from me that he had women. One day I'm driving down the street, and I run into my grandfather in his car with a woman I didn't know. I pull up next to the car, and I blow the horn and wave at him. He looks at me with this death stare and turns back to the road and drives off. By the time I get back to his house, I'm a little hurt because he did not acknowledge me, and, as soon as I walk in, he angrily pulls me to the side. 'Boy,' he snarls, "don't you *ever* motherfucking acknowledge me when I'm with another motherfucking woman! Do you understand me, boy?'

"And I'm, like, 'But, I'm your grand—'

"He cut me off. 'I don't *give a fuck* about you being my grandson. Don't you ever fuck up my shit in the street!' I can definitely say that he had some influence. But my dad influenced me, too. He was a real shitty individual. The reason why I say that is that he is a very, very good-looking guy and a man of power. He's a retired judge. When I turned eighteen, he said, 'I see that you're starting to date women and everything. Well, before you sleep with a woman, check to see who her father is 'cause she might be your sister.' I'm thinking, *This is the legacy that you pass on?* After that, I learned that my father's got something like twenty-three children, and I know only two of them. These were the two most influential men in my life when I was growing up, so I can see that my ways were cultivated from them." Even though Chris associates his father's infidelity with bad behavior and terrible character, he now repeats that behavior by cheating on his wife.

For many of the men I interviewed, the older generations seem to be doing a lot more to encourage cheating than their peers are. Men talked about having friends who supported their fooling around—either by helping to keep their secrets or by having affairs themselves—but this came after an older relative told them about this world. Robert, a media executive, said, "When I first got married, it felt like I got ushered into a new reality. It was like I went through a new door, and there were all these married men and older guys I looked up to who kind of said, 'All right, welcome, son, this is the backroom. This is where you can get up to a different level of manhood.' It was just shocking and alarming to see how normal it is and how prevalent it is for the higher-ups in society to say things that made it seem acceptable and even like something I should be doing. Like, I wasn't a man if I didn't."

A rare few said they were tacitly encouraged by a philandering mom. "I started seeing a psychologist to try to figure out why I was sleeping around," said John, a fiftysomething from Wisconsin. "When we got down to the root cause of it, some of it stemmed back to when I was a child and saw my mother cheat on my father. I guess I thought it was acceptable behavior."

Cheaters often enter marriage carrying the message that real men fool around, have more than one woman, never stop being wanted, and never stop chasing. They're also taught by many of the famous alpha men of society that being an alpha male means not being faithful. The stars of pop culture seem to be constantly cheating on their wives: Brad Pitt, Jay-Z, Jude Law, Tiger Woods, Ben Affleck, and on and on. One of my interviewees, Sam from New Orleans, said, "My dad was a huge Frank Sinatra fan when I was growing up, and you hear about how Frank had women in every city and was sleeping with other guys' wives and all that. I always kind of thought that was cool. Now, at my age, I've slept with dozens and dozens of women, and I've got a reputation among the guys, and I'm sure somehow I'm trying to live up to what Frank did."

Famous studs make infidelity look like an inherent part of being a big, powerful man just as Hollywood often makes sleeping around seem like part of being a real man. There are lots of movies about infidelity where people cheat and don't get caught—or, if they do, they don't lose their marriage and their dignity, perhaps leaving the impression that cheating is masculine, daring fun that doesn't ruin lives. Hollywood is like a little devil sitting on the shoulder of the typical American male, telling him: "Hey, man, live a little! Try screwing around!" Hollywood makes us feel like cheating is understandable—it's what real studs do, it's what people who are bored out of their minds do, it's what people who think that they've found true love do. And the film industry is so good at justifying cheaters' behavior that the overall effect of a lifetime at the movies is to view bedding multiple women despite being married as scandalous but normal.

Infidelity is a huge theme in the movies because it offers filmmakers a chance to pour sex, passion, secrecy, deception, drama, and tension into a single script. Cheaters and their stories are so compelling that even though Hollywood movies generally present a conservative brand of morality, the movies do not usually condemn the cheater as a horrible, immoral person because filmmakers need him too much. He's so important as the centerpiece of a wild story that directors and producers figure out ways to make cheating and cheaters seem sympathetic enough that they can be at the center of a story and not repel audiences. But iconic, popular films such as *Fatal Attraction*, *The English Patient*, *The Graduate*, *Brokeback Mountain*, *Goodfellas*, *Sex, Lies, and Videotape*, to name a few, show us affairs that are forbidden, and yet somehow acceptable to the audience. Of course, it's not as if merely watching a movie will spur a married man to seek some sex on the side, but a lifetime of movie watching *can* shape his views on infidelity.

This is an area where there's a major disconnect between the motivations of men and women in Cheatingland. Studies show that women who cheat tend to do so because they're dissatisfied at home, but that's not the case with men. According a study coauthored by psychologist Shirley Glass, an expert on marital infidelity and the author of *Not "Just Friends": Rebuilding Trust and Recovering Your Sanity After*

Infidelity, 56 percent of men who cheated said they were in a happy marriage, whereas only 34 percent of philandering women said the same. In their minds, the affair doesn't displace or denigrate the wife, it adds to the man's life.

"I know she would feel like the act of cheating and lying and sneaking is wrong," said Peter from Denver. "She would feel like it's an act of aggression against the marriage and not the act of someone who loves you. I get that. But that's not how I felt. I chased women, I slept with women, and I still felt love for her. Your wife becomes a part of you, almost a part of your body, and I can't not love her any more than I can't not love myself. Sure, she makes me mad sometimes— lot of times—but she's my home, she's an extension of me, she's my girl.

"It's like this: I may do shitty things to myself and to my body sometimes, but I still love myself. Cheating is, like, okay, let's get a greasy, sloppy double cheeseburger and chow down on that even though I know that it's bad for my heart, my cholesterol, my stomach, my weight, everything. But it tastes so good in that moment, and while I'm eating it, I'm not saying, 'Oh, wow, I have to run six miles on the treadmill to work this off.' I'm saying, 'Damn, this is a good burger!' Of course I want to live forever. Of course I want to be thinner. But sometimes I'm too weak to avoid the devil's temptations. Look, I feel the love for my wife deep in my body, it's immovable, she's baked into my DNA. I don't love my affair partner. I love getting sex from her and going home to my wife."

So, if they love their wives, why are they cheating? Sometimes it's to soothe a pain in their soul. Or it could be about feeding a need to feel dominant and masculine—humans are highly motivated by status and rank and several study participants said they were having affairs because they wanted to feel like they were at the apex of masculinity and more powerful than other men. They committed adultery to demonstrate their mastery of women and their rank above other men. To them, being big and bad enough to acquire multiple women proved their manhood. Or they could be dying to escape to a life that's far less demanding than their home life. In one sense, Cheatingland is definitely freer than Marriageland, with little to no responsibility. There's also this: for men who love adrenaline, excitement, and adventure, infidelity offers all three—an antidote for the sameness of marriage.

Larry from Chicago has been in one affair for a while. "The dynamics of something that's obviously forbidden creates a tension that is undeniable," he said. "It creates an electricity. You don't know when you're going to see that person, so the element of fighting for time together is powerful. If you're honest, it's hard not to get caught up in that. It's very exciting, it stimulates a great deal of your imagination. Still, you care for your spouse more. Way more. You love your spouse in a way that you would never love the other person, but that element of suspense that you feel all the time is powerful. The permanent spontaneity of the affair is intoxicating."

Some cheaters are responding to their marriage not meeting their needs in terms of sex, intimacy, attention, or ego boosting, but most of the time, a man's philandering is rooted in the issues and the baggage he carried into the marriage. Some men have a nostalgia of sorts for the sexual person they used to be, and they desperately want to reclaim that, whereas others have the opposite issue: perhaps they weren't very successful with the opposite sex before getting married, and now they want to experience what they missed. It's like they have unfinished business to address.

"What I really want is the acceptance of beautiful women," Mark from Las Vegas said , underscoring the notion that, for many men, gaining female approval is central to their self-esteem. "That was something I never got when I was younger. I just like beautiful, smart women, and I want to get accepted by them to the point where they would enter into the most intimate arrangement possible with me. Because that means, 'Oh, you're not the shitty little kid you were in high school; you're a much better person than that now.'" He's cheating as a way of trying to destroy the hapless boy he was decades ago and replace him with the attractive man he longs to see himself as now—an internal drama that his wife cannot resolve because it has nothing to do with her.

A distraught wife may yearn to know what goes through her husband's mind when he's sleeping with another woman. *Is he not thinking about me? Does he forget that we have a relationship, a love, a connection, a family that he's jeopardizing?*

The answer, painful as it is to hear, is: no. In fact, he's not really thinking at all. Once a man feels like he's on the verge of having sex, he's not able to think about much besides that. This surely had tremendous Darwinian value many generations ago. Robert, the media executive, said, "When I went after women, and I was alone with them, I had tunnel vision. All I could see was her. It was as if, for a moment, I forgot that I had a wife. I didn't *really* forget that, but I was able to push it into the back of my mind and just be alone with the woman in front of me."

Most of the men I spoke to said they were able to isolate themselves from the world, whereas most of the women told me they couldn't. It's like the male mind winnows down to sex, blocking out the rest of his reality. Over and over, I heard men say that when they're with a girlfriend or when a conversation with a new woman gets steamy, they aren't thinking, they're just acting on what feels like primal urges.

A man from North Carolina who did not give me his name said he loved going out to bars to meet women. "When I'm in that cheating situation, I don't think about the pain I could cause," he confided. "When I'm with another girl, I give that female my hundred ten percent attention, it's just me and her, and I let what I have to do the next day fall away. My problems—everything—just fade from my mind, and it's an oasis of just us two for that moment."

Jackson said, "My mind just goes blank when I'm talking to someone new. It's like, she floods into your mind, and your body takes over and says it's go time. And then your body is flirting with her, and you're just watching yourself go on ahead of you." Guys said that when they started thinking about sex, their mind got out of the way and their attention span narrowed sharply, as if suddenly their mind could perceive only one thing. They felt almost swept into a world where time slowed and all that mattered, all they thought about, was the woman they were with.

"When I'm alone in a room with another woman, my wife is not in my mind at all," said Jamie from Atlanta. "It's like I've gone into a secret room where I can't see her, and she can't see me—like I've stepped out of time and space and into this private nook where I can just snatch something I need for my ego and my body, and be another person, and then return to the real world feeling better about myself. Now, the second I leave that room, my feelings for my wife rush back in, and I feel shame and anxiety about whether she will she catch me this time, and I wonder how do I get back into my normal routine without having to answer awkward questions and lie to her?"

Robert: "Under most circumstances, it was not an intellectual decision for me. I wasn't thinking it through, it was more like my brain was blocked from thinking about anything but right now. I thought, *She looks good, I'd love to hit that, she's interested, why the fuck not?* The angel did not appear on my shoulder to explain why I shouldn't. All I could hear is why I should—until the next morning, when I ended up having shower confessionals, like, 'Lord, please help me, I'm sorry, please don't let me get caught, why did I do that, I promise, Lord, I won't do this ever again!' So, there was intellectual thought about it afterward, but during, once I see that girl and start to think I really have a chance with her, the background just fades away like in the movies, and this primal openness just rises up and takes over you."

This sort of bifurcation happens because humans have three separate systems for processing emotions related to sex and romance. The biological anthropologist Dr. Helen Fisher explained in a 2008 TED Talk titled "The Brain in Love" that the structure of the human mind is divided in a way that allows us to have feelings for more than one person at a time. She describes three main internal systems: (1) the sex drive that motivates you to seek multiple partners, (2) the romantic love that makes you want to spend your energy on winning over a specific partner, and (3) the deep sense of attachment that inspires you to stay with your partner in order to raise your children. But, Dr. Fisher says, these three systems do not always move in the direction of the same partner at the same time, so it's possible to have a deep attachment to one person while lusting after another.

We think of love as akin to a form of obsession, for when you're in love, you're supposedly unable to think of anyone else because your feelings about that person are dominating your mind. With new love the brand-new human connection causes the brain to release the neurotransmitter dopamine, associated with sensing pleasure and reward. But once you've settled into a long-term attachment, the love you feel can become like the wallpaper of your life. It's a fundamental part of you, and it shapes you, but it may not stop you from filling the holes in your life with a fling that lights your mind on fire but never reaches your heart.

In my study, so many people referred to cheating as an addiction that I realized there are clues as to why people cheat in the calculus of other addictions—because all of them are the same in many ways. In *Chasing the Scream: The First and Last Days of the War on Drugs*, journalist Johann Hari's book about the failed war on drugs, he theorizes that the root cause of adult drug addiction is having traumatic childhood events. Hari writes, "Child abuse is as likely to cause drug addiction as obesity is to cause heart disease." People abuse drugs as a response to the pain and the noise inside them.

I believe the same notion drives infidelity: many people cheat partly because they're in pain, usually due to experiences from before they were married, and having sex outside their marriage helps to soothe or block that pain. If a man sees himself as unattractive, he may crave affirmation for his physical appeal. If he feels like he's not as macho as his philandering father, he may reach out for other women to prove his masculinity. If he longs for a return to the freedom he felt when he had no responsibilities, he may seek an escape hatch. If he sees himself as not deserving of love, he probably won't tell his wife that; he'll just accept that his troubled marriage is all he deserves. He won't fight to change it, and he'll go out and find a girlfriend to help him achieve happiness. U

ntil cheaters fill that emptiness—until they get the attention, adulation, human connection, or whatever it is they need—like drug addicts, they'll run through barbed wire and virtually risk their lives to find the thing that quiets the malicious voice inside, especially if the high is intoxicating.

"To stop cheating is hard, man!" said Paul from Texas. "It's like drugs; it's that addictive. Especially if the side chick is not giving you any resistance." Ricky from Maryland said, "I don't know what my problem is, I just don't know. I've tried to stop. I've tried, I've tried, I've tried. I even tell myself I'm going to stop. But I don't."

In some rare cases, cheating is the active expression of misogyny and an outgrowth of a man's self-hatred, or his lack of respect for women, or both. Some men think so little of themselves that they disrespect women who love them. Or they think so little of women in general that they treat them as if they're disposable. According to a survey conducted by Dr. Ebony Utley, detailed in her 2019 book *He Cheated, She Cheated, We Cheated: Women Speak About Infidelity*, some philanderers also perpetrated physical, emotional, psychological, sexual, economic, and social abuse. She observed men who engage in psychological warfare intended to restrict their wives' freedom: isolating them through lies, gaslighting, or withholding money, thus giving the man control over her and the space in which to conduct affairs. In some cases, writes Dr. Utley, men used infidelity as a hammer to symbolically and emotionally batter their wives and show contempt for them. None of the men I interviewed admitted to such cruelty, but one of the limitations of a volunteer study is that you hear what subjects want you to hear. Even though my participants were very honest, by and large, I don't expect men to confess to me that they were physically abusive to their wives. But without a doubt, this happens, and Dr. Utley suggests that some men exhibit a disdain toward the women in their lives that's rooted in a deep-seated anger at their mothers. They know they cannot get even with Mom, so their rage toward her is transferred to their wives.

Dr. Utley also found that some men cheat because they're wrestling with the long-term impact of having been molested as children. In her research, she encountered several men who were sexually violated as children by family, family friends, or babysitters, and this has led to them becoming sexually permissive and open to cheating.

. . .

But even among men who love women, there isn't much love for monogamy. There is no prize in the proverbial locker room for being monogamous. The men in my study reflected the idea that monogamy is a price you have to pay for the opportunity to have a family. It's something they accept, but it's not something that many men want. "I don't think monogamy in itself is appealing," said Robert, who's made a commitment to be faithful. "Before I met my wife, I wasn't, like, 'I'm looking for monogamy!' I don't know any dude that's just, like, 'Monogamy's fantastic!'"

Having a family is great. Having a wife who makes you proud and is a friend you can rely on to help you build a family and enhance your life is fantastic. But most men say, if given the chance, they would rather be with multiple women at once. Cheating gives you a chance to visit that dream.

I asked almost every man in the study, "What can a wife do to stop a man from cheating?" and almost all of them answered the same way as Morris, from Cincinnati: "There's nothing a woman can do to keep a man faithful," he said. "It's not that I don't want her, I do. It's that I want something new. No matter how much I love her, she can't be a different person. She can't be new."

Many adulterers are driven by wanting more: more sex, more attention, more stimulation, more self-esteem, more affirmation, more proof of their masculinity. They're like people who don't know when to quit going back to the buffet again and again. "There's really no way to explain it other than greed," said Ray from Boston. "It's just greed. It's wanting your cake and eating it too. You want your long-term bond, but you also want that new-car smell; that rush of excitement you get with somebody new. You want the new passion, the discovery phase, the butterflies, the unmasking that draws you into someone new. It's some new thing that's thrilling. I think it's akin to getting drunk but still drinking more: you know you're going to feel bad later, but you do it anyway. You're, like, 'It feels good while I'm doing it so, here goes.'"

We all know that some men leave their families for their affair partner, but in my study, the overwhelming majority of participants said they would never do that. Lucas from Austin told me, "I looked at my side chicks like they were friends with benefits. I did not love them. My heart did not leap at the thought of them. I never wanted to introduce them to friends, I never thought, *What would life be like if it was just us?* Never. They were fun girls. They were for play-time, not real life. I was never dying to know how their day was going or any of that.

"Now, when my wife walked in the room, my heart would leap. I always have an involuntary positive reaction to seeing her that lets me know that I love her in a deep-down way. She's the sun around which my world revolves. My love for her is an involuntary part of me, like breath-ing. It's part of my operating system. But, you know, I still sometimes go out and do stupid-little-boy crap." In Shirley Glass's study, only 11 percent of men considered their affair a "long-term love relationship." For women, though, it was 40 percent.

Some might ask, If you want to sleep around, then why stay married at all? Because cheaters want both. One man told me he got married because he loved his girlfriend and saw her fitting into his life in a way that boosted him—but it didn't diminish his desire to have something more. As for Robert, who was having multiple affairs at the same time, "I've always been clear that I wanted to be successful," he said. "I wanted to build something, and I recognized that I was not capable of building something significant by myself. To do that, I needed a partner for real. If I'm going to build something and also have the picture-perfect family, I need a woman's help and her energy. But sometimes I was weak. I love the stability of marriage, and I love my wife, but I also like seeing if I can have sex with attractive women."

There's a sort of Peter Pan aspect to cheating. Buried beneath the mask of grown-up masculinity is the boy—or the twentysomething man—he used to be. Many cheaters have a close relationship with that younger self, and they listen to him as a guide for how their current lives should be. The young man in him loves acquiring things, which is the adult version of getting new toys. While some men limit themselves to cars or baseball cards, cheaters are often doing that with women. They're trying to score in accordance with the rules of big-boy culture, which looks at life as a competition for money, women, children, and cool stuff, and the man who dies with the most toys wins.

In this mind-set, they're using extramarital sex as a sort of playing field on which to compete with other men, or with themselves, or both. They're gamifying sex, trying to rack up numbers, pushing themselves to score more points than their friends or maybe more than they ever imagined they could have. For many, having both a wife and a mistress is an amazing bounty that makes them feel like a king, but a few need much more than that to feel fulfilled. Either way, cheating is connected to the male imperative to get more, more, more, which plays out in so many aspects of masculinity, from business success, to sports, to actual warfare.

Some cheaters are chasing women as a way to reclaim their younger selves. As we get older and grow into new stages of life, we move into new modes, activities, and responsibilities. The endless string of wild nights spent drinking, clubbing, going on hot dates, and sleeping around eventually turns into a stable relationship with brunching, double dates, trips to Ikea, and cuddling. This eventually morphs into family life, with late nights and early mornings spent trying to keep up with the baby, who's far cuter than you imagined and far more work than you dreamed. For some men, finding themselves on that last stage is both thrilling and frightening, and they may desire to escape, for a moment, from themselves.

In a pivotal moment in August Wilson's iconic play *Fences*, later made into a film starring Denzel Washington, the main character, Troy, confesses his affair to his wife and explains it by saying, "It's just, she gives me a different idea, a different understanding about myself. I can step out of this house and get away from the pressures and problems . . . be a different man. I ain't got to wonder how I'm gonna pay the bills or get the roof fixed. I can just be a part of myself that I ain't never been." It is liberating and exciting to step outside of yourself, get away from your everyday life, and try on new identities. Cheatingland is a place where you can explore exotic parts of yourself. This is one of the more invigorating, revitalizing, and seductive aspects of Cheatingland: it helps people see themselves in new ways.

CHAPTER THREE

THE FIVE TYPES OF CHEATERS

There are lots of similarities among cheaters. They tend to be risk takers, gamblers, and adrenaline seekers. They often have some sort of deep void in their lives and thus crave attention. They want to escape from being the adults they have become. But, of course, cheaters are not totally alike—there are variations. In my research, I found most adulterers fall into one of five distinct groups. Each one has a different reason for cheating and different ways of going about it. I call these groups Dead Bedroomers, Peacocks, Completers, Revenge Seekers, and Emotional Connectors. Let me tell you about each group and some of the members I encountered.

DEAD BEDROOMERS

The largest group of cheaters, Dead Bedroomers, are married people who feel like their love life has ended. The only thing going on in their bed is sleeping. Their bedroom is no longer the fertile place that produced the kids who in turn helped extinguish the flame. Dead Bedroomers typically say things such as "I want her, but she's always too tired for sex," or "I love my wife, I wouldn't trade her for the world, but at home my needs weren't getting met, so, you know, just take care of yourself where you can."

Even in private, men don't say these things with bitterness or blame—most do not see their sexless marriages as their wife's fault. They understand that her workload is immense and important—most of the Dead Bedroomers I interviewed respected the fact that their wife is busy and felt like she had a right to be exhausted because of everything on her plate. They knew that raising children was the most crucial part of the couple's life, and they were not resentful that their wife seemed to focus on that and paid less attention to them. One man broke down in tears, saying, "I miss the person I married." But he wasn't considering leaving his wife. He was wondering how he could get back the girl that he'd married. Meanwhile, he was trying to keep himself satiated both sexually and emotionally by having an affair.

A Dead Bedroomer longs to return to the relationship he once had with his wife and remembers what it was like being her priority. Many feel displaced watching the woman they love turn her attention and energy away from them and onto the children. It can be a bittersweet sensation. The affirmation these wives once showered on them has shifted away, and even though these men understand this exchange and love their children, they also feel forgotten. For them, cheating is a way of reclaiming some of the attention that they're missing at home. They're not taking revenge on their wives, they say, they just want to feel seen.

Most Dead Bedroomers tend to have one outside partner, and they often sound wounded and humbled, not angry or proud of their conquests. They don't look at their cheating as a way to boost their ego; for them, it's much more pragmatic. It's as if they're saying they have an itch and they understand that their wives are too tired to scratch it, so they've gone outside the marriage to find someone who will.

One Dead Bedroomer named Charlie said, "The intimacy has died down, and whenever I ask for it, it's 'Oh, I'm tired' or 'I'm not in the mood.' As a man, I don't feel wanted, and I have to stop asking because I'm constantly getting rejected— which makes me feel even less wanted. I'm not going to initiate if every time I do I get rejected. Cheating helps me not be mad every time she says no."

Dead Bedroomers feel under-loved, unfulfilled, and ignored at home, and they're trying to get whole. One Dead Bedroomer who didn't want to give his name said, "My wife is great. She's great with the kids. She puts a lot of attention toward them, and, obviously, when you put more attention toward one area of your life, there's a lack of attention in others. Then there's the stresses of work, and then there's my abuse of alcohol—not that I'm a drunk, but one drink at night ain't quite cutting it for me. So I tried to find other ways to kill that stress. That's what led me to go to that app Tinder. Over the course of the past year, just swiping left or right as a time waster has taken my mind off my stress. But then one swipe right led to a conversation with someone, and that escalated, and we met up and took it from there."

Many Dead Bedroomers said they feel beaten down by the mundanity of home life. They love their partner, but they're frustrated by what they see as the numbing routine of family life and the soul-crushing boredom that can come with it. They crave the break from routine and normalcy that Cheatingland offers.

"She's a wonderful woman," a Dead Bedroomer named Harry said about his wife. He's currently cycling through four or five affair partners. "I love her. She's attractive and all, but—this is going to sound bad—I've heard all of her stories. We've talked about everything. Marriage sometimes gets, you know, repetitive and redundant, and that's kind of difficult. I'm looking to be stimulated with new things, new ideas, new conversations." In Cheatingland, there are lots of new bodies, new stories, and new feelings, the antidote to the monotony of marital sameness. Where some men feel unexciting because their wives have heard all of *their* stories and the punch lines to all of *their* jokes, in Cheatingland he can find a new audience that will hear them with fresh ears.

Dead Bedroomers feel abandoned, and they want to solve that problem in the simplest way—which to them means avoiding a confrontation and conflict. Larry said, "She's moving toward being maternal and getting into children, and I'm getting into my career, and it's like two turntables playing the same song at different speeds and they're totally out of synch. It can be horrible. We've been together ten years, and there's kids involved, so separating would rip apart the fabric of everyone's existence. It's easier to just manipulate your reality. I don't want to create massive upheaval and financial trouble by leaving. Instead of all that, I just quietly sneak out the backdoor and go take care of myself."

As long as Larry doesn't get caught, cheating seems like the easiest way to solve his problems. For most men, it's less scary than launching into a major emotional confrontation about their issues with the relationship. If he insists on a conversation about that, he's going to have to summon the courage to say what he's really feeling, he's going to have to dig deep to find the words, and he's going to have to be vulnerable. Not only that, but he may hurt her feelings and have to deal with her retreating, or she may cry, or she may shut down, leaving the conversation stillborn. Having an emotional discussion about the state of one's marriage is challenging for a lot of men; they may not have the tools, things could go wrong, they could make things worse.

Therefore, to some, it seems easier to cheat and snatch some joy somewhere else even though this means he has to keep his lies straight, maintain a poker face, and manage the awkward complexity of having a separate life right under his wife's nose. In reality, it's *not* easy at all, it just seems that way at the outset.

One of the most interesting Dead Bedroomers I encountered was George, a factory worker from California who had a wife and four kids. We talked on the phone while he drove home from work. George described his household as chaotic. "I look at my wife, like, wow, she's very busy," he said. "We have no privacy whatsoever. If me and my wife have sex, it's a real quickie. Since we had kids, there's been no time for me and her to connect. It's pretty sad. I haven't had sex with my wife in three or four years." He still loves her, but without sexuality, something crucial is missing for him.

George said he'd been augmenting his reality with an office romance. "It's been going on a little over a year," he said. "She knows I'm married. She knows the whole scoop. We text a lot. We don't work in the same department. We don't want to make it obvious at work because people know that I'm married, so we're careful, but sometimes we'll both go on break at the same time, and we'll sneak away and meet up in the parking lot of McDonald's or wherever it's dark and go and do a little dirt right there." He said he's attracted to her but doesn't have feelings for her. That's typical of most cheaters—they're responding to their emotional voids by showing up for another person with only half of themselves present. George wasn't proud of all this, mind you, but he wasn't feeling guilty either. He said it was something he needed, and he felt justified taking care of himself because his wife was so occupied.

Men who were not getting sexual release at home said they considered their straying an acceptable choice under the circumstances. To them, cheating means taking their sexual frustration into their own hands and resolving the problem so that they won't poison the marriage with their dissatisfaction or resentment. If they can find a way to be okay with not getting it at home, then they can stay married.

"Cheating has helped me be better toward her," said Matt, a fortysomething married man from Raleigh who's been involved with another woman for six years. "Instead of banging my head against the wall, I found outlets, and that has allowed me to be more forgiving of her for not giving me what I need in that area. I don't feel resentful if my wife tells me no, which helps me be a better husband."

Dead Bedroomers are the lonely, lost souls of this study; the ones who feel abandoned at home and are looking for attention, physical contact, and a little affirmation to help them get through the day. For them, committing adultery is like marijuana—it mellows them out and distances them from the pain they feel. Many Dead Bedroomers said cheating allowed them to be at peace with whatever was happening (or not happening) at home. "When I dabbled, I wasn't frustrated no more," said Paul from Texas. "I would come home, and if she wasn't loving me, I was okay."

PEACOCKS

The sad, wounded-puppy-dog posture of a Dead Bedroomer contrasts sharply with that of the preening, strutting, swaggerific Peacocks, the second largest group of cheaters. Peacocks are voracious. They're gluttonous. They want to seduce and flex their sexual charm and score. They're the hedonistic party animals of Cheatingland, narcissists who need to be told again and again how sexy, seductive, and manly they are. They're guys with a high tolerance for risk and a craving for adrenaline and danger. One Peacock, Ray from Boston, said, "Less ambitious men don't cheat because they're more accepting of where they are in life. Truly ambitious guys want to travel and take risks at making money and are curious about everything; those guys want to experience all aspects of life, and that's going to draw them to the dark side."

Many Peacocks said that one of the best parts of infidelity was the risk. For them, cheating feeds them energy and boosts their ego—it is their cocaine. Ray continued, "I ski fast, I boat fast, I drive fast. I do a hundred twenty on the highway all the time. I know I could die, but I can't slow down. I spend too much money. I do stupid, foolish shit all the time because part of me is always trying to see where the edge is. Cheating is totally part of that."

Cheating is a big part of living on the edge. "When I get a new girl, it's like closing a big deal," said Jackson from Los Angeles. "It's like getting a big check. You get a charge from it. I just gotta push the limits and see how far I can get. I have to reach my hand into the fire to see how long I can hold it there before I get burned by the flame."

I named them Peacocks because in them I saw people who want to feel like they have the prettiest feathers in the entire animal kingdom. They need to feel attractive, desirable, wanted. They like to say to themselves, *I'm sexy enough to get lots of new women interested in me. I still got it.* They live for the chemical high from connecting with new women. James, from Oakland, described it this way: "You get that rush when you pull in a new chick. You get that intoxicating feeling. You feel like you're the man." Earning that sense of "I still got it!" is crucial for Peacocks. For them, every new woman they reel in affirms that they're studs, but they need that affirmation over and over. Whereas Dead Bedroomers are seeking a small amount of comfort and attention, Peacocks have a near-endless need to be showered with kudos and applause. That's why they have lots of partners. These are people who say things such as: "I've lost count of how many women I've been with since I got married."

Although Peacocks have a high opinion of themselves, they need validation from others constantly. Ben, a fiftysomething from Las Vegas, said, "I have at least four people that I have to talk to on the phone and check in with every day and let 'em know, 'Hey, I love you." I might say 'I love you' ten times a day. But who do I love? I only love myself. I look at it like I'm having four or five slices of pie every day." They acknowledge that having lots of affairs can be very stressful, but for them it's worth it because the attention informs their identity and confirms that they are who they think they are.

Having several people making a wild fuss over you seems to increase the sense that you're wanted and special. Peacocks thrive off of the ego boost of being desired by multiple people at the same time. Chris from Chicago who is married yet juggles several girlfriends, said, "I cheat because I think it's kind of deeply embedded in guys' DNA to do it. I can't help it, and it's fun for me. It's like a sport. I'll have sex with a woman once or twice—maybe three times if it's fantastic or she's really freaky—and then I'm pretty much finished, and I'm on to the next one. I need a new challenge, a new conquest. Just bagging the same chick over and over doesn't get me anywhere. And it has nothing to do with how much I love my wife. It has nothing to do with anything except I find it fun to have sex with new women." The swell of self-esteem that comes from the perspective of another conquest is what Peacocks are after. They want to see themselves reflected through the gaze of others as sexy and desirable because getting attention and affirmation at home isn't enough. In fact, no amount of sexual praise could be enough for a Peacock.

Some Peacocks are braggarts who want the world to know how badass they are—some of my interviewees even said it was fine to print their real names in this book. I didn't, but the fact that they were open to it shows you how brazen they are and that their rampant cheating is meant as a signal. But then other Peacocks are as silent as a sniper. Some have a good marriage, some don't. To them, the quality of their union isn't terribly relevant—they'd be chasing women whether their marriage was good or bad because they're trying to fill something that's missing within.

Brett, a fortysomething from Seattle who's in real estate, has had a string of girlfriends throughout his marriage. He said, "I love the stability of marriage. My wife is attractive, and I like having sex with her a lot. But I also like seeing if I can have sex with other attractive women. There's something fun about that." He said he likes "seeing if"—as in, what he really likes is *trying* to seduce other women. To Peacocks, the effort—the chase—is more important than actually being with a particular woman, They see seduction as a sport. Peacocks are so addicted to the rush from the chase that sometimes they don't care much about what happens after the catch. As Chris put it: "It almost isn't about the sex. It's to see if I can actually get it. Once I know I can get it, I don't really even have to go through with it. Sometimes just knowing that I could get it is plenty." Peacocks often describe cheating as a contest in which they're competing against not only against their past selves (*Can I keep up with what I used to do?*) but also other men (*Can I outdo them?*) and women (*Can I seduce and control them?*). "For me, it was more of a sport," said Jamie, a married man in Atlanta. "I was happy at home, but when I walked out of the house, I wanted to see how far I could get."

Peacocks like to feel powerful: they chose someone and got that person to say yes and do what they wanted. They do not want women who come easily. Robert, the media executive, likened his cheating process to "a hunt. Like, I wasn't a scavenger; I didn't want dead meat. If she's coming to me laying down, saying, 'Here it is,' I really was not interested. That shit didn't do it for me. I know some dudes that will just fuck anything. I needed the hunt; there needed to be some kind of challenge. I wanted to know that my mouthpiece is better than the next motherfucker's mouthpiece. I wanted to know I'm better-looking. I got more game. The challenge of the hunt heightened the senses and made it more desirable. Nothing felt better than the hunt. It made me feel like a man; it affirmed what manhood is supposed to be about. And, of course, there's dopamine being released as a result of the hunting in and of itself."

Chris from Chicago said he knows that if he paid for sex, never again would he have to worry about word getting back to his wife. However, prostitutes don't fulfill the core of what he's looking for. "I'm not interested in whores," he said. "If it were just about the sex, then maybe I would have had sex with some attractive young prostitutes, but it's not all about the sex with me. It's really more about the chase."

Some Peacocks confided that they were still chasing women the same week they got married—even that epic life event couldn't stop their hunger for the high of pursuing and catching women. Lucas, from Austin said, "I slept with somebody else maybe two days before I got married and somebody else a week after." Now, that's extreme: most Peacocks said the desire to cheat arose years into their relationship, perhaps because they began feeling uncertain about themselves and needed reassurance. Nathan, the actor from Cleveland, said, "You don't hear about a lot of people cheating three months into a relationship. You hear about them cheating after five or ten years. I think there's an inherent human desire to feel appreciated and to feel wanted and to feel attractive and all of that.

"Let's say you've been sleeping with the same girl for ten, fifteen years, and some of that sheen has rubbed off, but then the female trainer at the gym or the secretary at the office looks at you the way your woman looked at you fifteen years before. That's thrilling. You're exciting and interesting to her, so you're a little more exciting and interesting to yourself. That's intoxicating. That's a drug. 'I'm still cool. Yes!'

"I think people who cheat probably have both high self-esteem, because they think they can and should pull lots of chicks, and also inherently low self-esteem because they need it proven over and over," he noted insightfully. "If you had high self-esteem, you wouldn't have to go out and bag chick after chick to prove to yourself that you're still the man. But, you know, if your esteem is generated by the opinions of others, then you probably need to look outside your marriage to get the boost you need."

Part of what Peacocks get out of leaping from woman to woman is a constant return to the thrill of the honeymoon stage—that early part of a relationship where things are new and hormones are churning inside you. A love that's more mature cannot match the excitement of the buzzy honeymoon stage, and Peacocks cannot get enough of that intoxicating high. Ricky from Maryland, said, "I love that euphoria you get in the early days of first being around someone. I love that. I'm a serial relationship-ist, so, in my girlfriend's mind, I'm her man, and she's committed to me, and I got off on all of that. But once we really get used to being together and we settle in a bit, I'm gone, off to find someone new. I love that rush of excitement with somebody new. I love the discovery process, where everything about her seems new and awesome, and you've never had sex, or you've had sex only once but there's no routines—everything's still to be worked out. I think it's akin to getting a hangover and then drinking again. You *know* you're going to feel bad, but you do it anyway because it feels good while you're doing it. You're not thinking long term, you're just in it for the moment."

Some Peacocks say they're searching for the way to fix

some pain that happened long ago. Sam from New Orleans: "In my very first relationship, I was so lovestruck and so happy about finding someone that actually liked me, that I was dead loyal to her. I literally wouldn't lie to her about anything. I would be honest about things that I was ashamed about telling her, but if she asked me, I would tell her. I was super honest. If a girl looked at me, if I had a thought about another girl, I'd tell her everything. And then that relationship fell apart, she dumped me, and I didn't see the value of being that honest because, after all the trouble I went through to being honest, I still got my heart broke. And then I had a couple of very good friends in college that were notorious cheaters, and hearing about all of their exploits made me say, 'Why am I not doing it their way?'"

Many Peacocks said the pain they wanted to fix stemmed from failing with women when they were younger. Now that they were adults who had a better understanding of how to approach women, they were making up for that and assuaging the heartache from years or decades before.

Peter said: "I had my own issues. I didn't reach puberty until I was a sophomore in college, so I was always very short and was always very much looking like a boy. The things that happen in adolescence just hang with you so much. I was never able to get women or to even talk to women. I was very insecure. Then I met my wife, who's cool and beautiful. She taught me how to dress better and how to be stylish. She taught me so much.

"Then it was like, all of a sudden, I had all this fuckin' power! I was finally comfortable in my own skin. I looked good, and I felt good about myself, and that just opened up this whole other world that was never open to me before. Because of the person I was before and all the rejection and being ignored by women, now that they're checking me out, it's hard for me to turn down some beautiful young girl who let me know she was interested. It's hard for me to not pursue that." His wife would be hurt, of course—she didn't help transform Peter into a stylish man so that he could sleep around behind her back—but his infidelity was not a response to her, it was part of an internal conversation he was having about himself. It was about rewriting his self-image and proving to himself that he wasn't the loser he once was. But proving it once didn't solve Peter's deep-seeded insecurity; he needed to prove it to himself over and over.

Bill Clinton is perhaps one of the most famous Peacocks of all time. While he was president of the United States, he had sex with a young White House intern, Monica Lewinsky, sometimes in the Oval Office. This was both daring and foolhardy, as he was violating his vows as a husband and, when he later committed perjury in a deposition, his constitutional oath as a president in one of the most closely monitored positions in the world. Surely there's not a moment when there isn't someone with eyes on the president. This was a secret that was bound to slip out, and, after it did, it became a long-running national scandal that ended in his impeachment in the US House of Representatives in 1998. Political commentators reminded us repeatedly that "Slick Willie"—as an Arkansas newspaperman had dubbed him in 1980 during his first term as governor—was the sort of guy who loved to get into trouble and then figure out how to get himself out of it as a way of showing himself and the world how smooth, how smart, and how charismatic he was. For so many men who cheat, that sense of getting into crazy situations and finding ways to turn them around is part of the joy. For them, it makes life more interesting and makes them feel smarter and more badass when they're slipping in and out of dangerous situations like a secret agent whose mission is to seduce women without his wife finding out.

In Clinton, we can see so much of the typical cheater's personality. He's narcissistic and thinks the world of himself—that man sure loves the sound of his own voice—but he's also deeply insecure and in constant need of mountains of affirmation. Clinton was a politician who needed the love of the crowd like oxygen. He's a Peacock who seems to have chased women for the ego boost and the re-re-re-confirmation that he was charismatic, powerful, and desirable. He was gluttonous in his fast-food diet and in his pursuit of women who happened not to be his wife.

During his first presidential campaign, in 1992, Clinton's adulterous past came tumbling out of his closet. When the door finally burst open, a parade of blondes emerged to say they had slept with him since his marriage to Hillary Rodham, who called them "bimbo eruptions." In his wife, he had a brilliant, powerful lawyer with keen political instincts who enhanced his status and helped him win elections, but, behind closed doors, he had a string of women with huge, blonde hair. It seems like Hillary Clinton was a permanent and essential part of his world—they celebrated their forty-sixth anniversary in 2021—but obviously he also wanted interactions with the opposite sex that were entirely different from his relationship with her.

It's not uncommon to find the world's most famous men behaving like Peacocks because the drive to be hyper-famous is about needing the love of many, which is the essence of being a Peacock. Another US president, Donald Trump, who cheated on all three of his wives, is perhaps the world's biggest narcissist, the world's biggest martyr, and a man in constant need of reassurance of his status. Deep down, the former president is a real estate developer from the outer borough of Queens who always wanted to be accepted by Manhattan high society, which can feel like the center of the world, the elite of the elite. But Trump lacked the class, intelligence, seriousness, and self-control to get there. Still does, in fact. His affairs seem to be fuel for his ego, feeding his need for self-gratification and a way to cover up massive insecurities.

Golf legend Tiger Woods, too, was a Peacock—a powerful man who'd conquered the sports world and was pursuing an endless string of women while married, seemingly to perpetuate the sense that he was powerful and alpha.

Tiger may have been seeking to rewrite his past: old friends remembered the young golfing prodigy as somewhat geeky and sweet, far from the ladies' man he would become. But as a globally famous multimillionaire, he was an alpha male able to command women in a way that young Tiger could have only dreamed of.

Interestingly, a 2021 HBO documentary about him, *Tiger*, revealed that Earl Woods, Tiger's domineering father, was a voracious cheater who often slept with women in a Winnebago camper he kept parked next to the golf course where teenage Tiger spent most of his time practicing. Earl set the example: this is what a real man does. Not only that, but a golf pro who mentored Tiger also let the teenager know that he was cheating on his wife. Like so many cheaters, Tiger grew up idolizing older men who showed him that having extramarital sex can be a part of a man's life.

COMPLETERS

Completers, the third largest group of cheaters, are tied to one specific outside partner by an almost mystical thread. Completers are the poets, the philosophers, the romantics of Cheatingland. They have interests or feelings that are too intense for one person to fulfill. They truly love their life partner—fact is, completers talked about their love for their spouses more frequently than men in the other groups—but there's also one specific person in the world they can't pull themselves away from. This is someone who connects them to a part of themselves that their primary partner cannot help them reach. Completers feel they need a second relationship in order to fulfill or complete their whole selves.

Completers want someone who is the yin to their wife's yang. "My wife and my affair partner looked totally different," said Morris from Cincinnati. "They had totally different personalities. They liked to do different things. One was more of a partier who wanted to hang out all the time, and the other was more of a homebody who liked to play games, so it's like a Frankenstein girlfriend. You get to pick and choose what you like about everybody and have it all at your disposal. One was better in bed; one was smarter and more fun to talk to. I had all the bases covered. If one of them wouldn't do something, the other would." I initially thought of somehow using the word *Frankenstein* to describe Completers because they seem like they're trying to piece together one perfect relationship by splicing together two or three different ones—they want "to Frankenstein" the ultimate woman. A Completer sees his spouse and his affair partner as two parts of one perfect partner.

There are different subtypes of Completers. A man may have an interest that means the world to him that his wife doesn't share, and so he'll bond with a woman who is willing to experience it with him. This could be sexual—perhaps he likes to have sex as a furry—or not sexual at all. Maybe he loves European cinema, and, in going to those films, he meets Sarah, who loves them too, and she helps him develop that side of himself.

A Completer affair might involve a woman from the man's past—perhaps a former high school or college flame—reintroducing him to the young, carefree person he used to be years ago. Sometimes it's an old relationship that ended, but the feelings never died, and the chemistry remains strong.

Whenever we fall in love, a chemical reaction occurs that makes us focus on the new person to the point where we can barely think about anyone else we've ever dated. However, with Completers, there may be a love from the past that's so durable it survives the intrusion of new love. Here's a scientific analogy from outer space: most meteors that enter the Earth's upper atmosphere burn up, appearing merely as streaks of light in the sky. A rare few of these rocky objects, however, survive the journey and strike the Earth's surface as meteorites. Well, if your marriage is the Earth, then your love is like the upper atmosphere, vaporizing potential objects of affection. The Completer's affair partner—that one person he can't turn away from—is that rare meteor able to penetrate the bonds of your relationship and embed itself right in your heart.

Although most Completers are satisfied with one outside partner, others prefer ordering in bulk (so to speak). Harrison, a financial industry executive on the East Coast, considers himself a multifaceted personality who needs to have different women to satisfy each of his sides. "In my main relationship," he reflected, "I have the woman who I thought would be a good, safe partner in life, which mainly meant she wouldn't do anything to hurt me emotionally. But in the women I chose as satellites, I sought adventure, danger, and being pushed out of my comfort zone. Generally, it wasn't about sex, it was about having a different experience. I get to play out different parts of me with different women.

"I have the woman whom I take to classy restaurants and treat really nice, and she's, like, 'Oh my God, you're so intelligent and worldly.' Then I have a girl who satisfies my dark side. She's strictly reserved for 'All right, let's go to a bar and get shitfaced and do cocaine and fuck in the bathroom.' I am literally compartmentalizing myself in each relationship."

Whereas Dead Bedroomers and Peacocks are out for sex with anyone who makes them feel better about themselves, Completers prefer sharing emotions with a particular person. Thus, they tend to form stronger bonds with their affair partners. From that foundation, they can build a true relationship, not merely an illicit fling, which means that their betrayal will be seen as much more traitorous and insidious. Some spouses can find a way to forgive their husbands for sleeping around if it was purely for sex, but it's much harder to forgive your partner for having a substantive relationship with someone he's truly connected to.

The most famous completers of all time are surely Elizabeth Taylor and Richard Burton, the legendary actors who met in 1962 on the set of the major Hollywood movie *Cleopatra*. They were both married (Liz for the fourth time, on her way to eight in all), yet both recognized instantly the intense chemistry between them. In 1964 they divorced their spouses and married each other, launching a passionate and turbulent love story that lasted for many years. They divorced in 1974, remarried in 1975, and divorced again the following year. Yet they remained intensely close friends until the end of Burton's life in 1984, indicating that, on a deep level, they could not be apart from each other—even if the highest hurdle to their relationship was each other.

REVENGE CHEATERS

If Completers are more romantic, in that they are led astray by what they love about life, then Revenge Cheaters are their opposite: they're driven into Cheatingland by rage at what life has shoveled their way. They're highly motivated, intense, furious, scorned people who are dying for payback. More than anything, they're in pain.

Steve from New York was faithful for years until he figured out that his wife was cheating on him. He was deeply hurt—his self-confidence destroyed—but instead of confronting her, he just started going after other women. In Steve's view, "I think people who have revenge affairs, and maybe this is not an okay thing to actually say, but I think we're damaged."

Revenge Cheaters are probably unfaithful because they got cheated on, but they may also be taking revenge for some other relationship crime. Many of the male Revenge Cheaters I met had not been cuckolded—instead, they tended to be vengeful over affronts that had nothing to do with sex. Many were weaponizing infidelity as a response to feeling emasculated, such as Eddie the engineer.

"My wife was doing things to undermine my masculinity," he explained. "Like, she knew I had one rule in the house: I don't want our kids to see us argue, so, if we do, we excuse ourselves. She never did that. I always had to be the better person and shut my mouth to keep the peace. Even if I did, a lot of times she would continue dogging me in front of my kids while I'm biting my lip to the point where she was making me look like less than a man in front of my children. She was maligning my masculinity. I couldn't accept the way she would talk to me in front of the kids. If she got upset, she didn't care who was around; she would go off on me. I was, like, 'You're cutting off my balls.' I couldn't have that. Finally, I said I'm going to retaliate. I used my sexual prowess to pay her back." Eddie slept with her sister.

Another man, Paul, told a story that was far more disturbing. Before his wife even did anything that could be said to provoke him, when their relationship was young and unblemished, he cheated on her with a friend of hers. Paul chose that woman specifically so that if he and his wife ever got into a fight, and she hurt his feelings badly, he would still have a bigger bomb to drop on her. It was like he was taking out revenge insurance or secretly stockpiling ammunition for war.

"If she says some wild shit, I will say what I gotta say," he told me. "I got this in my back pocket for an emergency: 'I fucked your friend. What's up now?'" He was lying in wait, holding back the fact of his betrayal, just in case the moment came that he wanted to ambush her with his vengeance card. Paul is consumed by and directed by anger over something that has not yet happened in his relationship. Perhaps he was hurt in a prior relationship, so he's preparing to take revenge before the affront even arrives. He could not say what had happened to him to make him feel like he had to preemptively prepare a nuclear strike against his wife. Who had hurt him so badly that he felt like he had to be ready for war? He intimated that he slept with her friend not for the fun of it, and not for the ego boost, but for the power it gave him over his wife.

It reminded me of how husbands and wives can fight with a ferocity that outstrips all of life's other pairings—neither siblings nor sworn enemies can be as cruel, as horrible, and as petty to each other as a pair of bitter, enraged spouses. No one has the power to hurt you like your wife or your husband. But even amidst all that, this man stood out. It sounded like Paul actually *looked forward* to a future argument so that he could destroy her. I never heard anything else like that in my research. This was callous, violent, feckless—and perhaps sociopathic.

I never heard anything else like that in my research, but surely he's not the only guy like that. No group of cheaters has a burning hot sense of anger and pain like Revenge Cheaters. They talk as if they've had a chunk of their soul ripped out, and now they're hurt, dazed, and lashing out. Revenge Cheaters are ambivalent about cheating because it's not really their thing; they've been thrust into this life, needing some way of exorcising their anger. They do it as a reaction rather than as an expression of who they really want to be. Cathy, a female Revenge Cheater, said, "I was going behind his back and doing a lot of deceptive, hurtful things, and I was saying, 'This is not the type of person that I want to be.'" Nevertheless, she persisted.

EMOTIONAL CONNECTORS

Emotional affairs can creep up on you quietly and suck you in deep before you know it. Like carbon monoxide gas filling your home, they're invisible killers. Emotional Connectors have friendships that are sexually charged, extremely intimate, and platonic, but just barely. The man and the woman look like close friends, they meet in public places, they may even let their spouse know that they're spending time with this person, and they are definitely not having sex, but so many other aspects of passionate relationships and secret affairs are present. They're flirting. They're saying romantic things to each other. They're telling their partner stories they don't tell their spouse. They're keeping the true depth of the relationship hidden from their spouse, and when they're at home, thinking about their dear friend makes their heart race—a sure sign that the friendship has crossed over into something more. They may not be giving up their bodies, but they're sharing something far more intimate: the heart.

Despite the fact that emotional affairs aren't physical, they're still devastating to the loyal spouse. In my research, they do not usually evolve into physical affairs (though it's possible for them to become Completer or Dead Bedroom or Revenge affairs), but they are arguably more dangerous than any other kind because they are based on a deep and intense emotional connection. The partners are simulating a loving relationship without the excuse of craving a physical release.

No one sets out to have an emotional affair. It usually starts quietly, often without the two parties even realizing it, but the next thing they know, they're entangled with their coworker, or their neighbor, or their friend, and their blood is pumping at the sight of that person, and they're thinking about them all the time, and their marriage is at risk. Most of the study participants who spoke to me about emotional affairs were women. A few men said they had engaged in them, but most weren't even aware of their existence. Surely there are some men involved in emotional affairs, but perhaps they don't think of them as betraying their vows. Meanwhile, many women who were in emotional affairs referred to themselves as cheaters.

Ex-lovers who remain friends are definitely at risk of falling into an emotional affair. Phil, from San Antonio, said, "I never physically cheated while I was married even though I had several relationships that my wife did not approve of, such as some of the women that I had been with before we were dating. After we got married, my wife really didn't want me talking to those women, but I still talked to them secretly."

Many emotional affairs develop in the workplace. "First, we started running into each other at lunch," said Tony, who works in Washington, DC. "Then we started making plans to go to lunch at the same time, and then I started bringing her little breakfast gifts in the morning, so I'm walking into the office with a coffee or a croissant for her, which means I'm thinking about her before I even get to the office. I could feel myself becoming obsessed. At that point, I wouldn't think about her when I was at home, but as soon as I got in the car to go to work, I started thinking about her and counting the minutes until I felt it was not too early to text her.

"One day she said that I was her 'work husband,' and she giggled, and I thought it was the cutest thing I'd ever heard in my life. At first, I thought, Yes, and then: Oh, fuck! It was like my brain warned my heart, 'You're not supposed to feel like that,' and my heart said, 'I can't hear you!' I was in so deep that I couldn't pull back."

Soon Tony was spending half of his workday thinking

about his 'work wife' and sending her instant messages and wondering what he could do to get and keep her attention and strategizing about how he could make her smile. It was not a situation he would want to discuss with his wife or his boss. But he was able to rationalize that he wasn't doing anything wrong because he'd never touched her. With nothing sexual happening, he could delude himself into thinking that he and his colleague were just really good friends. That allowed them to grow far closer than they should have. It never turned sexual, although their habits of touching each other on the forearm and the way they groomed each other were more intimate and exciting than they should have been. Tony said he did not know about the concept of an emotional affair until after they stopped working together. But he had wondered why the good-bye lunch they had after their co-employment ended had felt like such a breakup lunch that he had wanted to cry.

· · ·

Most forms of infidelity fall into one of these five common types, even in Hollywood films. The sad Dead Bedroomer with the soulless, empty marriage is at the heart of *American Beauty*, which won the Oscar for Best Picture in 2000. It revolved around a Dead Bedroom marriage between Kevin Spacey's Lester Burnham and Annette Bening's Carolyn Burnham, who exude resentment and mutual disgust from the first moment we see them. They never enjoy each other for more than a few seconds, and we can't imagine them sleeping together. Lester echoes many of the Dead Bedroomers in my study, longing for the carefree woman his wife used to be.

He laments, "Whatever happened to that girl . . . who used to run up to the roof of our apartment building to flash the traffic helicopters? Have you totally forgotten about her?" But *she* is the one who cheats: in pursuit of career success, she sleeps with the king of local real estate, Peter Gallagher's Buddy Kane. For Carolyn, their passionate hotel sex is like a confidence injection, and, immediately afterward, we see her driving in her Mercedes, dancing in the driver's seat, looking rejuvenated and feeling sexy enough to flash a traffic helicopter.

Hollywood also loves the peacock sex God who needs a virtual harem to feel like he's the man he's supposed to be. In *Goodfellas*, Martin Scorsese's 1990 mob classic, we follow Ray Liotta's Henry Hill, a man on the rise to the elite level of his Mafia family. Of course, he's got to have certain things to indicate his status: a big Cadillac, a diamond pinky ring, and a young *goomah*, or mistress. He puts her up in an apartment, then starts sleeping with her friend, acquiring lovers to prove to himself and others that he's a stud. Classic Peacock behavior.

Fatal Attraction, the 1987 erotic thriller classic, is a Completer affair in which Michael Douglas's Dan Gallagher loves his sweet, demure wife, Beth (played by Anne Archer), but he's seduced by her total opposite: the wild-hearted erotomaniac Alex Forrest, played by Glenn Close. Alex is the yin to Beth's yang, and together they seemingly give Dan the entire spectrum of womanhood.

Brokeback Mountain (2006) is also built around a Completer relationship: both Jake Gyllenhaal's Jack Twist and Heath Ledger's Ennis Del Mar are married to women, but they give each other access to a side of themselves that their wives cannot help them reach. It's not just that the two of them are gay in a rural world where being homosexual can get you killed. They don't just want men, they want each other. To them, their best days are the rare ones they get to spend together. It's as if they were born for each other. Their love is so intense that they talk about it as if it's a force that's greater than them. They complete each other's lives—with each being the other's only person in the world who makes life worth living. When Ennis says, "I just wish I knew how to quit you," that could be the Completer's motto because for them, relationships are more than a desire, they're an imperative.

In Steven Soderbergh's 1989 drama *Sex, Lies, and Videotape*, Peter Gallagher's John Mullany engages in a twisted and torrid revenge affair with Laura San Giacomo's Cynthia, the sister of his wife, Andie MacDowell's Ann Bishop Mullany. It's a way of getting back at Ann for being so uninterested in sex. John is an arrogant, entitled, unctuous caricature of a successful businessman, who wears suspenders all the time and drives a BMW. He knows that of all the women in the world, Cynthia is the most forbidden, and he seems to enjoy sleeping with her precisely because it's so taboo.

Emotional affairs aren't seen very often in Hollywood movies. After all, what's the cinematic value of an unconsummated affair? But comic actor Chris Rock's *I Think I Love My Wife*, from 2007, is built around an emotional affair between his character, Richard Cooper, a married, suburban father with two young kids, and his old friend Nikki Tru, played by the stunning Kerry Washington. In her first scene, she wears a tight dress, flirts, and disses the concept of marriage. She's the wild free spirit that he's no longer able to be, and she's reminding him what it was like to be young and unencumbered. Richard lets Nikki take him on an adventure, but despite all the sexual tension and flirting and desire, they never have sex. But it definitely looks and feels like an affair, and he knows it.

"It's not like we're fucking," Nikki says.

"It is *like* we're fucking," Richard says. "The only thing is, we're not fucking, and I feel all the guilt as if I'm fucking you without any of the pleasures of actually fucking."

• • •

Each of the five subtypes of cheaters is in need of something different in his life. When you know which of the five a person is, you can start to see what he was looking for and what he needs. That doesn't mean you can stop him or that you should forgive him. But if a wife understands what she's dealing with and what her husband wanted out of an affair, she can begin to comprehend what he is saying through his infidelity and decide how to respond. Some wives take their husbands back, some dump them, and some have affairs of their own.

CHAPTER FOUR

THE WOMEN OF CHEATINGLAND

My study is about men's infidelity, but over my years of research, I met several women who cheated, and I realized they deserved their own chapter. In some ways, their experiences as adulterers were different from the men's, but there were also some key similarities. Women tended to be better than men at telling their stories and identifying their whys and their motivations. Most of the women gave me their first names, none gave me their last names, and three preferred total anonymity. One of the biggest differences is that whereas men often cheat while still emotionally invested in their marriage (because they have a desire to have two or

more women), women tend to cheat when they are emotionally through with being married. It's as if having an affair is
a warmup for checking out and moving on.

For example, take Molly. She felt like her life was in a rut.
She was depressed, and her marriage was not giving her any
joy. She was done fighting to make it work and was considering divorce. That's when she met someone. "I got infatuated
with this one guy," Molly said. "I was working on a small team
in a fairly large company. We worked long hours in a very intensive environment, and you can easily grow close to people.
This guy, who was also married, got infatuated with me, and
it just grew faster than I could realize. We would go out drinking after work, and one night, after drinking, we ended up
making out in the parking lot, and that's how things started."

The affair made her happy. "It was exciting," Molly said.
"It was new, and, because it was illicit, when I was at home—
bored to tears and not connecting with my husband—it just
lent a certain amount of energy to my life that wasn't there
otherwise." Many women said they started cheating after
emotionally abandoning their marriage; even if they felt like
they couldn't get divorced, in their minds, they were done
with the marriage, so they didn't feel guilty about their affair. They said that part of what they were doing was using
the affair to help rebuild themselves. For example, Molly was
revived by her affair. "I feel alive," she said, "and I haven't in
a very long time."

Many women said that their marriage wrecked their

self-esteem, but having an outside romance helped them reassemble their confidence and shore up their sense of self. Susan, who was in a lesbian marriage, said, "It did give me more confidence in myself and in my ability to kind of control my own life, which was being taken away from me in all reality. I think that, in the long term, it gave me the confidence to end the relationship on the terms that I wanted to end it on." Molly said, "I had to be brave enough to end my marriage, and cheating helped me do that. It just made me feel alive again and attractive and worthy and sexy and happy and strong." She felt like her lover helped her see herself in new ways. "I drew on his strength to get me through the end of my marriage," she said. "I was kind of wounded, and he fed my ego and gave me strength. He made me excited about myself. He made me excited about life again."

Women also say that it takes less subterfuge for them to pull off an affair than it does for men One thing that most men never think they'll find in Cheatingland is their wife. Erika, a thirtysomething married woman in the Washington, DC, area, told me, "I had my affair partner over to the house while my husband was at work. I knew it would have taken my husband an hour and a half to get back to our neighborhood. There's no such thing as five minutes away in DC. Plus, I knew he would never have expected it."

Women cheaters break down according to the same five major groups as men. Erika, for example, was a Dead Bedroomer. As she recalled, "I found myself so miserable in my marriage. You know, men tell you about themselves, and women, we don't listen when people tell us who they are. I mean, we were dating in college, and I had to do an interview for my French class and write the interview in French. I interviewed him, and one of the things he told me was, 'I'm kind of an asshole.' And I remember my professor saying to me, 'Are you sure you want to be involved with this guy?' And then, lo and behold, after we had our first kid, his asshole tendencies came out strong, and I got very unhappy." Erika's home life was dragging her down so she used an affair to grab herself the happiness and self-esteem that she wasn't finding at home.

Molly was married for years and unhappy. She said, "One day I woke up and looked around and realized that I had been married forever and that meant I'd been living someone else's life forever, doing everything my husband wanted to do. I wasn't who I was or who I wanted to be. Then I found someone I connected with, and it just happened."

This is fundamentally different from the motivation of Kathy, a happily married Peacock from Indianapolis who gets a lot of love and affirmation from her husband. "I cannot say a bad word about my husband," she said. "He's smart, he's cute, he's funny, he's hardworking, he adores me. He is a great dad. He takes care of his body. He's an excellent lover. I am married to, like, Mr. Wonderful in so many ways." Nevertheless, she's having an affair with a guy at work. And this is not the first time she's strayed.

"It's such a rush to be wanted by someone else," said Kathy, who is in her forties. "It's a really big ego boost to have pure, uncut desire coming at you from people outside your marriage. That sort of affirmation and attention and ego boost is totally a drug that I can't give up."

Peacocks tend to have self-confidence and bravado, but we can see their insecurity in the way they go so far out on a limb to find validation. Kathy said, "I want attention from someone who isn't my husband. When my husband tells me I'm beautiful, that's nice, but if I hear it from somebody else, that's even better. I know that isn't right, but knowing that it's wrong makes me want it even more. Seeing myself through the eyes of another guy makes me feel young and sexy. I couldn't stop myself from wanting his attention if I tried. And believe me, I've tried. I would have these little breakups with my whatever you call it—'affair partner'—but then I would think to myself, *You know, I really miss what that relationship brought to my life.*

"I wonder sometimes if it's because I am, like, at the cusp of maybe losing my attractiveness, which has been with me through my whole life. It's been easy to get men's attention. I'm cute. But as time goes by, as a female, you realize that your cuteness is not going to last forever. I really needed to feel that again. To be reminded that men still want me. I mean, when it started, it was like, hey, here's this superhot, funny, smart, intelligent guy who likes me, and when's the last time somebody liked me? I'm, like, forty—nobody likes me anymore. Guys don't even look at me. But this guy is super fit, he's got this amazing body, and to have this super-hot guy be interested in me was really flattering.

"And I remember it escalating so slowly that I thought to myself for months, *If he would just kiss me, then I would be fine.* Like, if we would just kiss, this would stop. And then that happened, and I started thinking, Okay, *I just want to fuck this guy once, and that's it.* And then it's like I've been dragged into this big, long, ongoing saga. I mean, I really fell into it; I wasn't looking for it. We would instant message on our corporate network and talk all day, and then we would do little stupid things together like get a coffee or whatever. Then one day, I can't remember why, but I gave him my phone number. I remember thinking to myself, *There's no way I'm going to your house for your birthday party. I have like a major crush on you.* But then he's making little jokes like 'That's why I crush on you' or 'You're going to be my next wife,' and being wanted by someone like that was so enticing. It feels good. And you buy nicer underwear, you work out more, you make an effort in what you're going to wear. Having somebody out there who's interested in you and having that feeling that you haven't had since you were, like, twenty, is just a really interesting kind of dynamic. Yeah, I feel wanted by my husband, but that's not really the same. The newness and the electricity of it coming from someone else is powerful. It's like a drug almost sometimes. Sex is just sometimes hotter with somebody that you haven't been with for a decade."

Mary, a married woman from the Pacific Northwest, was a different breed. She's a Completer. Her affair is happening right under her husband's nose—he knows the guy, and Mary knows the guy's wife—but it's a relationship she feels she needs. Mary's younger brother was killed in the Iraq War, and they were extremely close. This is why she's enmeshed in a long-term affair with her brother's best friend. She says she's not someone who would normally cheat, but this relationship fulfills a gaping hole in her. "After my brother died, we got close because we both missed him so much," Mary explained. "We felt connected because we shared this intense grief."

Although she loves her husband, she needs this second relationship because it keeps her feeling close to her brother, thus completing her world. Her husband did not know Mary's brother, so he can't help her stay connected to her brother the way her affair partner can. She said, "It's really nice to talk about my brother with someone who really gets it and just to be around someone who feels his absence acutely the way I do." Of course, they don't cry about him every time they see each other, but when they're together, his presence is tangible, and the memory of him is alive. "My therapist says if I let go of my affair, it will feel like letting go of my brother all over again. He could be right." She conceded that they don't need to have a sexual relationship, but the feelings between them are so strong that they do. Their bond is wrapped up in who she was as a child—this man is a deep part of her personal history.

"I've known him since I was twelve," said Mary. "That's when he and my brother became friends. The three of us hung out for a long time throughout my teenage years. If my brother hadn't died, this probably wouldn't have happened," she said, "because we probably would not have become this close again." He's such an enduring and important part of Mary's life that she doesn't even have to hide him from her husband.

"It's like hiding in plain sight, honestly. My husband knows that he and I are close, so if I'm, like, 'Hey, I'm gonna go hang out with him,' it doesn't faze him. He's fine with it. We've spent a lot of time in the past socializing with him and his wife, so, on the surface, it just appears like these are people who are close, and there's not a reason to think there's anything else going on." This is what being a Completer is about: there's an emotional tie bonding the two. Completers said there's probably only one person in the world whom they'd cheat with.

Jill is a Revenge Cheater who had an affair because she felt she had to return fire. "I did it because my husband did it first," she told me. She sounded hurt and weary, , and cheating became the weapon she used to reclaim herself. "I found out that he had been having multiple affairs, including one that lasted six years. I was devastated and angry. The day I found out, he stopped cheating, expressed remorse, and said he wanted to stay married and keep our family together, and would do anything to do that. But it was all very difficult for me to process. One day when I was very, very angry, I got on the dating website Ashley Madison. I thought, *I'm going to talk to* one *person.* I wasn't intending to have it actually go anywhere. I just intended to blow off steam and feel like I had gotten even in a safe way. But within twenty-four hours, I had over a hundred responses, and I started reading through them.

"I replied to one—don't ask me why—we ended up going out, and I started my own affair in an effort to understand what he did and also to get back at him. I was so angry that I started seeing this guy mainly out of anger, but he helped me heal from some of the things that my husband had done, and he helped me understand what my husband did."

"I think it's natural that when someone hurts you, you want to hurt them back," said Jill. "I would be lying if I said there wasn't an element of satisfaction for giving it right back to him. As ironic as it is, I think doing this helps me deal with what my husband did. The person that I'm having an affair with understands me because he went through infidelity with *his* wife, where she cheated on him, so it's helping both of us heal from that wound."

Jill's having fun with her fling even though it does require a little work. "We'll drive an hour away from our city to have dinner. He said, 'Look I want to hold your hand. I want to give you a kiss. And I don't want to have to look over my shoulder. I just want to have a nice evening with my girlfriend without having to worry about it.' So, we drive an hour or two away just to have dinner. But we always have to have some story prepared. We would play "What's our story going to be if we run into somebody?" And then we'd have to memorize today's story. Which was kind of fun but kind of stressful."

From my research, a lot of women who fool around on their husband are in emotional affairs. This might seem like less of a betrayal, but the way that an emotional affair links two people's hearts and minds makes it a very serious threat to a marriage. One lesbian named Nina said that because her special friendship wasn't physical, she was able to lie to herself about the affair until it was too late.

"My marriage was nine years old, and it was getting a little stale," Nina said. "I'm really extroverted, and my wife—well, my ex-wife—she's really introverted. I wanted more freedom, more stimulation, more activities, and she wanted to be more of a homebody. Plus, with the kids, every night I'd read them a book before bed and then fall asleep with them. My wife would complain, 'Hey, when is it my time?' But I didn't know how to turn in a flash from mommy me to romantic me. At first, I had no idea how to do it, but after awhile I had no *desire* to do it. So, things were getting worse and worse.

"Then one weekend, I went away with a group of girls. I was telling someone about how disjointed I felt at home and how I didn't feel the freedom I wanted, and as I was saying this, there was this woman sitting nearby, listening and nodding, like she agreed. I felt like she got me. After the weekend, this woman and I started texting. At first, it was light stuff, like, 'Did you see this article in the news?' But it kept getting deeper. I was sharing news stories, great photographs, and funny jokes not with my wife but with her. I was giving my friend the best parts of me rather than giving them to my wife. I thought I had a fun, exciting new friend. I did, but soon I had much more than that. I kind of hoped that it would just go away—like I could get it out of my system and come to my senses—but I couldn't pull away because I felt like this woman understood me in a really profound way.

"So we kept texting all the time. Texting so much that my wife would ask, 'Who's texting you?' I started hiding our relationship because, by then, I couldn't stop. I'd bend over backward to find ways to fit her into my schedule, to be near her office so we could grab lunch or coffee three or four times a week, while never telling my wife I was seeing her. It really took on a life of its own. The relationship became an unstoppable force, and I became weaker and weaker to stop it.

"She was looking at me with virgin eyes and loving my stories and seeing the magic in me. This woman was looking at me in ways my wife hadn't looked at me in years, and that was very hard to resist. I was a sucker for the way she looked at me; I'd do anything to see that. She said, 'You're amazing,' and when you haven't heard that in a long time, it's the greatest gift. It was all so intoxicating. I had such a skip in my step.

"But my wife is very intuitive. She recognized what was going on. She said, 'You're having an emotional affair!' I said, 'No, we're just good friends.' I assumed that affairs were physical by definition, so if we weren't fooling around, then there was nothing wrong. I tried to make it about my need for freedom. I said, 'Are you saying I'm not allowed to have a new friendship?' But she knew it was more than that. She demanded I have no further contact with her whatsoever. I felt that was unfair and unjust and overly controlling. I'm not your child who you can boss around, and I'm not touching her, so why do you have the right to tell me I can't even talk to her?

"But I was lying to myself. I was fighting for the right to talk to her because I felt a part of me coming to life again thanks to her, but I was essentially cheating. Deep down I knew she was right. I never wanted to end my marriage over it, and I didn't realize that it had the potential to wreck it, but I let things get too far because I was clinging to the idea that it wasn't an affair because it wasn't physical. But what we were doing was definitely an absolute betrayal.

"One night my wife finally cornered me and made me come clean about what we'd been doing, and I heard myself recount everything: all the texts and lunches and conversations and sharing. When I heard myself say that I needed her in my life, I knew that I was having an affair. After that, my wife left me."

• • •

Women, like men, said that forbidden sex was an incredible allure. "The hotel sex was more thrilling," said Molly. "We were doing something wrong, and we knew we were wrong, and we were getting away with it. So that was thrilling. My heart used to beat so fast when he would drop me off at my house. But it was worth it. Great sex is always worth it."

Women had an even easier time compartmentalizing their behavior, as if entering Cheatingland were like stepping through a portal to another dimension that allowed them to be new people. For instance, one woman confided that she doesn't let her husband tie her up during sex because it's too stressful to do that at home. What if the kids suddenly need her in the middle of that? But when she's off in a hotel with her boyfriend, she loves letting him tie her to the bed because in that space, she feels free enough to give up control. She enjoys using the cheating space to do things that are scary in real life. It's liberating and exciting to step outside of yourself, and Cheatingland gives people that opportunity.

One of the biggest differences between male and female adulterers was that where most men don't feel guilt or regret and have lots of ways of justifying and rationalizing their behavior, many of the women I spoke to could not shut off their guilt about the affair. Even though they are emotionally disconnected from their marriage, they may still feel bad about doing something wrong—which is echoed in the fact that some of the women I spoke to would not even share their first names. One woman who insisted on remaining fully anonymous said, "At one point, my husband tried to have sex with me after I had just had sex with somebody else, and I just cried. He was, like, 'Why are you crying?' I couldn't tell him, but I felt like such a whore. I felt terrible that I had just been with [her affair partner], and then I came home, and he was trying to have sex, and I felt gross and lame and ashamed to be in that position and to be turning him down because I'd already been with my other guy. Just the thought of both of them being in me—I felt terrible. I felt guilty. But I couldn't tell him why because you can't ever tell that you're cheating. You have to keep that lie. You have to keep that secret."

Whereas men think of their affair partner as someone they can easily detach from, a woman can sometimes sink her feelings into her lover so deeply that he becomes an important part of her life; a trusted friend whom she needs to touch base with if life goes bad. Needless to say, that can be complicated, as Kathy, from Indianapolis, recalled:

"I was in Atlanta last week, and I ended up in the hospital ICU for two days. One of my girlfriends has my other guy's number, and she knows that if anything ever happens to me, there's this other person that I love. So, she had to text him at, like, ten thirty at night and be, like, 'Hi, I might not have the right number, but so-and-so is in Atlanta and was just admitted to the hospital for xyz . . .' That's *not* how you want to get news about your loved one, like you're a third party. Not cool. But he knows that's how it has to be. It just reminded me how crazy all of this is. It's just a mess. I really love him, but I can't be there for him like I want. What if something really bad happens to him? I can't be there? One of his best friends got really sick with cancer and suffered for ten months and then died, and I couldn't sit with him and console him like I would with anyone else in my life. If you can't be there for somebody when they're going through all that, then what kind of friend are you? Even though we're so close, we're so separated. It's really weird."

Kathy had a Peacock's sense of bravado, but at the same time, she also had an overwhelming sense of anxiety. "I had to get super shady," she said. "I got a separate bank account, and I diverted money without it being noticeable. But then I worried, like, O*h my God, what if my husband is trying to refi our house or something, and he runs a credit report?* Having a secret account is such a tip-off. I'm well aware of the risk I run, and I've thought to myself that this is going to end badly. It's always in the back of my mind that this shit is going to blow up in my face, and I'm going to end up living in an apartment with a cat.

"Another problem is that I've told too many people. I told two of my close friends, and that never should have happened. And one of my friends then told her boyfriend, who, of course, knows my husband. I know that will blow up in my face one day. If my husband asked me, 'What the hell is going on?' I don't think I'd be a very good liar. I don't think I'd be able to deny it very convincingly.

"At one point about a year ago, my husband thought I was sleeping with a *different* coworker, and I felt really bad for him because I think he recognizes the disconnect in our marriage, and he saw this guy that I had become friends with, and he linked those feelings, thinking I was cheating with him. I was like, 'No, nothing's going on with that guy,' and because it was true, I was able to deny it. But in the back of my mind, I was, like, *Right smell, wrong tree.* I'm a mess."

The chaos of Cheatingland gives these women both positive and negative feelings about themselves. While most men revel in the crazy details of their affairs and the attention it brings them, many women confessed to feeling constantly torn. They love how desirable and sexy it makes them feel, but they may also feel bad about the whole thing. A woman who wouldn't give her name said, "It didn't make me feel good to lie and cheat. I made up a bunch of stories: I was going to hang out with my friends, or I needed to go to this party, whatever. It was scary how good I was at it. It was thrilling and scary at the same time. I had a young child, so that was scary because, you know, I'd make up all these stories just to get away. I would sneak out, and my husband would be at home with the baby, and I felt good but also horrible at the same time. I knew he suspected something was going on, which was scary.

"He actually caught us one time when we were sitting outside in a park, having some food. He came up and said, 'Are you fucking my wife? Are you having an affair with my wife?' I was so embarrassed. He confronted us, and, of course, we denied it. 'Are you crazy? You don't know what you're talking about!' We denied it, and I got upset, like, 'How dare you question me!' He backed off and apologized, and that crisis was averted.

"It could've been the end of my marriage. It could've been the end of my life. But I calmed my husband down and made him think nothing was happening. But when you lie, it leads to another lie and another lie, so I had to tell him more lies, which made me feel horrible. But by then, my husband was like the enemy. He really didn't deserve any respect or any compassion because he was so mean to me. He was abusive. He yelled at me throughout my pregnancy. He was horrible. And the only reason I didn't leave is because I didn't have my money. I couldn't get away, I was trapped, and I had a permanent frown mark in the middle of my forehead because I was unhappy all the time. The only happiness I got was from my affair, but it was a huge source of anxiety too. Well, my husband was really the source of anxiety, but, at that point, it's the same difference."

Whereas many of the men who cheated seemed to pat themselves on the back and compliment themselves, most women could not. Men often left Cheatingland and returned to their primary relationship feeling refreshed and ready to deal with any rejection from their wife. Women, on the other hand, said they often returned home and saw the issues and problems of their marital situation with even clearer vision.

"You know what really sucks?" Kathy said. "It's when you have a good time in your secondary relationship, and then you have to go back to your primary relationship, and you have to act like everything's okay. You have to be, like, 'Oh, honey, what's for dinner?' I'm so fucking sick of playing 'What's for dinner?' It's like this is all we do. Like, I saw that one tweet that said all marriage is just like a series of texts back and forth asking if we need anything from the grocery store. Yes, we have to be good at life management and family and finances and all the adulthood stuff, but where do blow jobs fit into that equation? I sure don't know. In marriage, everyone's too fucking tired to make an effort, and it can drive you insane when you think about how nice and easy your affair is."

Women cheaters are often pulled in two directions: thrilled with the infusion of self-confidence from their affair yet also grief-stricken about deceiving their husband and the sorry state of their marriage. The affair is a source of both happiness and pain. They couldn't just forget about either one. Jill, the Revenge Cheater, said, "I would never recommend to anybody that they do this. I am grateful that I met the person I did, and I'm glad for the experience that we've had together so far. But my husband hurt me, and then he was hurt by what I did, and just because he did it first did not make it okay for me to do it back to him. And all of the deceptive, hurtful behaviors I did, that's not the type of person that I want to be. An eye for an eye leaves the whole world blind. It can be fun and exciting to have an affair and have sex with somebody who's different, but there's a lot of stress in having a drawn-out affair like this."

One serious hurdle faced primarily by women is getting away from their children long enough to have secret time with someone. Even if a woman hires a babysitter or drops off her kids with a friend, she's still on call. Mom never knows when the kids will suddenly decide they absolutely need to talk to her right now about homework that's due in three days or a fight over which show they get to watch before bed. Sometimes they just need to hear Mom's voice to go to sleep.

One woman solved the problem in a way that no one should try. This mother gave her kids the over-the-counter cough and cold medicine NyQuil before bed, so that when her lover arrived, the kids would be knocked out for the night and wouldn't disturb them. She essentially drugged her children night after night in order to conduct the affair. That is not how most moms would ever manage their family. But many women said children can become a wedge, driving a married couple apart—the work that goes into parenting can easily turn into resentment if the other spouse doesn't pitch in to do his fair share.

A woman who declined to give her name said, "We have a special needs child and my husband was completely no support during the whole incredible stressful period of figuring out how to address her needs, and because of that my husband and I kind of grew apart. To this day, he hasn't been to a single appointment with my daughter—or *our* daughter, I should say. He doesn't know any of the specialists involved in her care and there are many.

"That was my first What-am-I-doing-with-this-person? type of aha moment. Then my sister passed away, and instead of trying to redeem himself, my husband was shitty, and I expressed to him that he wasn't supportive. He was really disconnected from the whole situation and just left everything on me to do. It was really crazy for him not to support me in, like, the worst time of my life and be just completely disconnected. After my sister died, that was the straw that broke the camel's back. I was, like, 'Okay, I've been faithful for— what?—seven, eight years now? It's time to go ahead and do me. Time to make me happy. And that's what I've been doing for the past two years."

At first, this deeply unhappy wife and mom sought nothing more than someone to bed. "It was like, 'Hey you, you're handsome, you think I'm attractive, let's bump pelvises,' is how she put it. "But now I'm in a more significant relationship," she said. "We talked on the phone on the regular for about three months, and then we said, 'Okay, let's go out together,' and going out turned into relations."

Where most men tried to minimize conflict in their affairs so that things didn't blow up and ruin their lives, sometimes people—well, listen to this from a woman who had become pregnant by her lover:

"When I got pregnant, he was, like, 'Keep it!' I was, like, 'No, I'm gonna do the right thing and not bring any more shame or anything into the world.' So, I fixed that, and I was, like, 'You go your way, I go my way, do not contact me.'

But he was, like, 'Oh no, I love you, I love you, I love you. I can't let go of this relationship because I'm in love with you. You don't understand.' I begged him to leave me alone, but he didn't listen. He kept contacting me and dredging up feelings and telling me he loves me.

Or this: "One day I said to myself that the only way I'm going to get rid of this dude is if some shit hits the fan. I had my friend go on Facebook and tell his wife everything. Then there was an explosion. It really was like feces everywhere. She was livid. I know because I heard all about it because he was still trying to be with me. He was texting me blow-by-blow accounts of what was going on. It was mayhem in that house for a while. She'd be sitting on the couch beside him, and he'd be on the phone texting me and begging me not to leave him. He didn't know *I* was the reason why she knew. He thought one of my friends had taken it upon herself to tell her. He didn't know that I'd put everything in motion, and I didn't tell him.

"I got a random text from somebody talking about how I'm a bitch and all this stuff. I knew it was from the wife because I don't have any enemies. That's when my *Love & Hip Hop* inner persona came out. I bought an ad online that listed her phone number and said that she does sexual favors for free. After that, I know her phone was ringing off the hook. I don't feel good about it now, but at the time, I was in my feelings. But I know she was freaking out. I heard all about that too. Then I texted him and said, 'Oh, by the way, I'm still pregnant, so get ready for child support.' I *wasn't* pregnant, but I just wanted to add an extra jab in there. I wanted him to be freaking out, too.

Or this retaliation against an ex-lover and his wife:

"I called Child Protective Services and said that, as a concerned citizen, I wanted them to go to their house and do a well child check. I told them that they were living in a one-bedroom apartment with five kids, and she suffers from depression, and I think he was doing cocaine in the house, and it just didn't seem like a suitable home for kids. I convinced myself that I was doing the right thing, that I was doing my civic duty and looking out for the kids, but, really, I just wanted to wreck their lives. But, yeah, they did a wellness check. It was hell."

Female philanderers are like men in that many of them are inspired by their cheating fathers. Erika, from Washington, DC, said, "I never had any intention of ever cheating on anybody in any relationship. In fact, I was quite adamant against it because my dad had cheated on my mom, and these women were so nasty and aggressive to my mom. She's the one who's got first position, you know what I mean? But these women would call the house and terrorize my mom, and I guess that was probably my undoing because I had to, I guess, learn to have some compassion for people who did cheat. I still think you should keep your folks in line; they should not be disrespecting your home, disrespecting your wife. They gotta know their position. I can understand the

French model of having affairs: if you're going to have one, keep your folks in line. They should respect your home." Erika would grow up to have her lover come to her home for sex while her husband was at work.

As we've touched on, some men have fathers who encourage them to screw around outside their marriages. By and large, women do not have their mothers and grandmothers pushing them to commit adultery. But as the number of women having affairs rises, so does the number of women who may advise their fellow females to go ahead and do it because, "Hey, it worked out for me when I was in a situation like yours." This could have a normalizing effect for many women and perhaps lessen the guilt a little. Women who stray seem to carry the guilt that society imposes on them regarding sexuality and sexual agency. On the other hand, men who cheat are buoyed by the message that it's cool to have a harem, it's good to be a stud—men have an almost endless list of justifications for why sleeping with other women is okay.

Many women said they rely on their extramarital activities as a passive-aggressive way of confronting their problems with their marriage. They're not running from the relationship, or from themselves, the way that many male cheaters do. Instead, they're trying to force a conversation. Nina cheated on her wife after their marriage started to fall apart, but not because she wanted to leave. She still wanted it to work and part of her plan was to make them talk.

"I think what I was missing was that communication with my partner," Nina said. "After a long time in a relationship, you get comfortable, and you get lackadaisical, and you take each other for granted, and you're just not nice to each other. I was trying to talk to her and reconnect, but our day-to-day life is busy, and my attempts would go over her head." Another woman said cheating was about getting her wife's attention. "My affair was like me trying to address the problems in my relationship by taking a nuclear bomb and putting it in our living room, and detonating it to force something to happen."

CHAPTER FIVE

THE CHEATER PERSONALITY

What if you could look into the future and know before you got married that your prospective spouse would be unfaithful one day? What if you could see it coming? Well, after talking to a lot of cheaters, I noticed that some personality traits are fairly consistent among them. If you are aware of them, you may be able avoid someone who's more likely to break your heart down the road. For most men, cheating is like a recessive gene. The attitudes and influences that make a man feel inclined or justified to go out and break his wedding vows have already cast their spell on him before he marries.

Now, does marriage change people and make them into

cheaters? I have not found that to be the case. Dead Bed-roomers, who are responding to the pain of a marriage not going quite the way they want, usually had it in their mind before tying the knot that it was okay to cheat if necessary. In fact, most men who cheat entered into marriage with a per-mission structure in their minds that allowed them to cheat. They've come to a fork in the road where the relationship has gotten bumpy, or they've begun to dislike their midlife iden-tity, or they're doubting their masculinity, or they're feeling a strong desire to be affirmed by someone new. And when they get there, they activate the justification system that was instilled long ago that allows them to put aside any guilt they might have and cross the boundary into Cheatingland.

There's not one strict, absolute predictable set of traits that all male cheaters share, but several studies (including mine) have demonstrated narcissism to be

one of the most common and reliable predictors. Philan-derers tend to have a high sense of self-regard and oversized egos. They usually consider themselves good-looking and smart and entitled to love and attention. They believe they deserve a little more from life than other men. They want to drive fast, eat gluttonously, and corral multiple women as a way of reminding themselves that they're a cut above other guys and have the power to seduce the opposite sex. For men who think they're good-looking, if that's an important part of their self-image, they may need to be reaffirmed and re-minded of that from time to time. The older that men get and the further away they drift from being young and virile, the more affirmation they may need.

"I've always been known as a pretty boy," said Zac, an actor. "In high school and college, I was always one of the guys that girls would talk about. When I started acting professionally, my looks were always talked about. It's not that I was full of myself—I was just used to people responding to my looks. But as I got older, I noticed I was hearing less and less about my looks. I wasn't always the cutest guy in the room, or whatever. Which made me feel like, 'What the heck?' If I didn't have that, then who was I? I felt drawn to find women who would give me that attention and tell me one last time that I was a pretty boy because that was a part of me that I didn't want to let go." Some cheaters are surprisingly insecure, and a compliment from an attractive woman, or even just attention from a woman, is a powerful currency for them.

According to Zac, "When a woman tells me I look good, I'm cute, whatever, or just gives me that look like she's into me, that is everything. That puts a charge in my battery and a pep in my step. Okay, *I still got it!* I don't even need anything to happen to get that jolt. Just knowing that she likes what she sees is enough to make me smile from ear to ear." In some ways, the cheater is like the retired athlete who still longs to hear the crowd roar for him so that he can feel like he's back on the playing field, soaking up that adoration. Women who respond to him are like the crowd cheering to tell him he's still *the man.*

For a man to pursue women without being stymied by a fear of hurting his wife, he must be self-centered and have a low level of empathy or a very quiet conscience. Adulterers are usually impulsive, good at compartmentalizing, quick to chase self-gratification, and slow to realize the potential consequences of their actions. Most cheaters fall on one edge of the sociosexual scale, which is a way that sociologists measure how willing people are to have sex without love. People who are sociosexually *restricted* require commitment, intimacy, and love before sex. People who are sociosexually *unrestricted* are comfortable with having sex without love, and they're open to having sex with people they don't know that well. Most cheaters are sociosexually *very unrestricted*, and this is, again, a trait that's typically developed well before marriage.

In my study, I heard cheaters talk about their wives as if they were the furniture of their lives. I use that word in the sense of a fixture, a permanent piece, an important part of the home that is an extension of the self. Therefore, to them, a wife's being the furniture of his life meant that she is an essential part of him. And so they felt free to chase other women, secure in the knowledge that their partner would never leave them even if she found out.

But for other men, seeing their wife as furniture meant that she is something so commonplace, they don't pay attention to it anymore. Something you take for granted. They love their wives, but they tossed that love into a remote corner of their hearts awhile ago, and they don't really think about it that often. So, they sneak around without really considering what losing their wife would mean. They feel justified. They don't feel guilty. They don't feel like bad guys. They think they have a right to do this.

As Nathan the actor said, "I treated my wife great, never abusive, didn't argue with her much. I was a good dad, took everyone on great vacations. I was a good dude when I was with her, but when I was away, I would stray. But, honestly, I didn't equate getting laid on the road with being a bad person."

A lot of men believe that cheating does not make them bad guys, because they separate home behavior and street behavior as if they're two different realms. Jamie, who's had a string of affairs, said, "Whoever I'm with, I take care of them. But even the best of them is not going to make me behave." Many men feel like their role in the family is to be a provider, and if they do that and take care of everyone, they're entitled to sleep around. "I was coming home on a Tuesday night at three in the morning smelling like Jameson whiskey and pussy and cigarettes, and feeling, like, *It's cool*, 'cause, *hey, I pay the bills around here*," Jamie said. "I never said that verbatim, but that was in my mind."

Many cheaters love adrenaline. It's one of the constants throughout their lives. They're not averse to pressure, competition, and high-stakes games. As I found, many of them have jobs or serious hobbies that demand the ability to handle pressure. They tend to enjoy outsmarting people and getting away with a plan and deftly making their way through emotional minefields. The thrill of meeting someone new, the delight of being affirmed, and the ecstasy of illicit sex—as well as the anxiety about getting caught after they return to the real world, and the frenzied effort to keep it all quiet—the entire roller-coaster rigmarole is catnip for them. These are guys who, in many cases, have a twisted sense of humor. They're people who would find something funny in an insanely messy situation. They're men who would have their mind overtaxed, their phone buzzing like crazy, their lungs still fatigued from yesterday's strenuous, uh, workout, their spirit pulled in two directions, their life as madcap as a Shakespearean comedy of errors, and they wouldn't freak out. No, they would laugh deep in their soul.

In his heart, the adulterer likes having a fuss made over him. He enjoys being the center of drama, he finds the insanity of the cheating life fun. "It's just a rush to see if I don't get caught," said Christian from Miami. "I liked the danger. The way my heart pounded when I was with her made me feel alive." These are men who love a challenge, who want adventure. They're easily bored, and they love having an outrageous story to tell their closest friends. They are guys who like to break rules and test boundaries. People who don't do whatever society tells them. They feel like they're special somehow. Exempt. They feel like they can run the red light, cut the line, cheat on their taxes, and get away with it all.

They like getting over on everyone and showing themselves how slick they are because they think they're smarter and badder than the average bear—and in many cases, they are.

To survive as a cheater, a man can't be sloppy. He's got to be scrupulous, circumspect, analytical, and calculating. He's got to have a reliable memory and occasionally be able to see around corners. When he's got a secret friend, he's got to think about how to keep her happy without alerting anyone that there's some outside force in his life. If he usually comes home from work tired but then suddenly starts skipping through the front door, clearly proud of himself, his wife will likely notice the shift and question it. Or if his mistress gives him grief or dumps him, he can't go home and be in a funk. Either way, he's got to be able to tamp down his feelings and keep them to himself.

Of course, that means he's creating a whole intense emotional ecosystem that he's keeping secret from his wife—excited before dates, ecstatic while alone in a room with the other woman, elated as he floats home from a night of mutual lust, or angry when there are complications. Hiding all of that will push him further away from his wife. He's having a whole separate life and dealing with a torrent of feelings that he's not sharing with her—and he's already in the habit of not sharing his emotions with her. It's harder to connect with her when he's doing so much behind her back.

A lot of cheaters struggle to connect because they're unable to communicate effectively, or they can't find a way to talk about the issue they really want to discuss. They're trapped in the idea that real men don't talk about their emotional problems. They just pacify themselves and keep on trucking. One married man said, "I was coming home, and I was literally just sitting in the driveway not wanting to go into the house. I didn't know why I was so miserable. And one day I just started cheating, because I was grabbing at some kind of pleasure, joy, something."

You might think that someone who's in pain and feeling like he has holes in his soul that need to be filled should tell his wife. That's part of being in a partnership, right? Some men say they try, but men are less likely to do the hard work of communicating difficult emotional messages and more likely to stuff that pain into a box and find a quick fix.

Many men told me they tried to ask their wives for more sex, but communicating about the subject was often tricky. Greg, from Baltimore, said, "Over the years, there've been times when I've been very, very open with my wife about my unhappiness in this area, and that leads her to kinda go into a shell and not want to do anything at all. So, I learned that I really can't say anything at all about it. If my wife does something with me, great, but I'm not going to sit around hoping that she realizes two months have gone by and we haven't done anything intimate. There was definitely some resentment and bad feelings and anger that came out, and it was all around my feeling like 'Why can't you do this for me? Why can't we have sex more?'

"I mean, if you are my only choice sexually, and you refuse to have sex, or you ration the amount of sex you're willing to have, or you limit what we can do to a very boring, vanilla list, then am I just screwed? Do I just have to accept the amount of sex that the person who wants it less is willing to have? Do I just have to accept that she's only willing to do three or four things, and some stuff I want to try is totally off the table—forget it, no interest, don't bring it up—because then she doesn't feel like having sex at all? I can ask her for more, but I can't ask too much, I can't push, because what happens then? Do we end up having sex while I'm wondering if she doesn't really want it, or she's thinking about her guilt about not having sex enough, or she's all up in her resentment about feeling guilted into having sex, or . . .

"All of that is just gross. I know she would not want to hear this and would freak out if I tried to tell her, but I think cheating has actually opened me up and made me into a better partner. Because instead of banging my head against the wall, I found outlets that allowed me to take care of myself so that I could be more forgiving of her not wanting to give me what I need in that area. When I have a girlfriend, I don't feel resentful if my wife tells me no. That helps me be a better husband."

Several men said they had tried to talk to their wives about their concerns, only to find that did not help. "I don't find a lot of glory in what I do," said Shawn, a fiftysomething from Maryland. "If somebody were to put my feet to the fire

and say, 'Why do you do it?' I would say I almost feel justified
to do this because I have tried in numerous ways to broach
the conversation with my wife. But every time I try to bring
it up, it ends up doing more harm than good. So, I had to find
a way to take care of myself."

When men say they need more sex, they're often talking
about much more than sex. For many men, not having sex
means feeling unseen, unloved, unwanted, and unmanly. But
all that's hard to admit. Men sometimes feel like it's inappropriate to say, "I need more sex." Several guys said that no matter
how much they want more sex from their wives, they would
feel horrible saying, "Hey, when you're done running through
the one million things that the kids need from you today, can
you find a little more energy and have hot sex with me?"

Charlie from Tennessee, said, "I don't want to push the
issue and say I need more because I know the relationship is
built on more than that. But that's something that I need. But
she's a hardworking woman. She's always here to take care
of the kids and work extra hours and do whatever is needed
for her parents and everybody else. So, I mean, I don't want
to be pushing the issue super hard after she's been grind-
ing to help everybody and keep stuff in order everywhere
else. Even though, you know, that is a need that I need met."
Charlie sees her holding up the family like Atlas, and he re-
spects her for that, and so he struggles to see his feelings as
legitimate even though he can't dismiss them. But he's craving sex, intimacy, and attention immensely.

Marriage is filled with all sorts of compromises: spouses will often go to a restaurant or a movie they don't really like or a party they're too tired to attend just to make the other person happy. But doing that with sex is unacceptable. No man I spoke to said his wife should have sex when she doesn't really want to, nor should she perform sex acts she doesn't really want to do. They wanted her to *want* to do these things. But if she doesn't, then what? Having sex is critical to men feeling like men, and if they're denied it, then their sense of self is at risk. But is it just . . . oh well? Is there nothing they can do?

If a spouse refused any other task, it would be outsourced immediately. Let's say the husband cooked dinner every night, and then one evening he announced that he was no longer going to do that. His wife would call DoorDash or Caviar and let the chefs at some local restaurants do the cooking. If a wife refused to shop for groceries—"I cannot set foot in Whole Foods once more; I hate that place!"—then they'd contact Instacart or Fresh Direct and let someone else shop for them. But what if a partner says explicitly or tacitly that they are not really interested in sex anymore? Or they are not into a specific act? Sex is an incredibly important part of marriage. Can a partner outsource their sexual needs?

Some men make up the difference by going to strip clubs or watching porn—those are socially acceptable alternatives for some, but those options don't really solve the problem for many men. He really should communicate his needs to his wife, but that's very hard. And even if he could say, "Hey, can we have sex more often?" he may feel awkward being any more specific than that. How do you say, 'Hey, so . . . we're having sex, like, once a month or less. Can we bump that up to once a week or more? And can we not do quickies? And can you do more fellatio, and can we try this sex toy I've been looking at . . .? Can a couple really negotiate sex like that? Most married couples can't promise each other that they're going to have sex on a certain date, at a specific time, and for this long, "and we're going to do that thing you like, and . . ." Lovemaking is supposed to be a free expression of bodies and feelings, and once couples start dictating some sort of contract, it loses that freedom, that spontaneity, that passion. Who wants to be in the act and have his wife thinking, *Okay, he asked me to do that thing, and we haven't gotten to that yet, and we've been at it for thirty-five minutes, and he wants it to go at least another twenty minutes, so I should start soon because . . .*

That's not sexy. That's terrible. It doesn't bond you two, and it doesn't work. If you are two working parents, then it's even harder to make sure there's some weekly sex—every morning there's rushing, every evening there's exhaustion, and no matter how old the kids are, parents never know when they'll come wandering into the bedroom or when they'll yell out from another room, so they can't totally relax. It's hard for many couples to talk about what each person wants from their sex life, and many men said they were afraid of expressing their unhappiness to their wife for fear of hurting her feelings and/or attaching some stigma to sex that may cause her to shut down about the whole topic.

Men said the amount and quality of sex they have at home is very important to them, and not having a satisfying sex life is deeply frustrating. But they also said that not getting what they want sexually is definitely not enough of a reason to leave a marriage. Matt from Raleigh said, "In my time with my wife, the one area that lacks is in the bedroom. We have children, and she's a good woman and supportive, so I feel it would be totally backward to leave just because of sex. It's kind of the eighty-twenty rule: Why would I leave over a bad twenty percent when the other eighty percent is good? So, I just use cheating as a way of supplementing what I don't have." Some guys feel that taking their sexual needs elsewhere is the way to have it all: the nurturing home life they need and the active sex life they want. Cheaters say that if their wife isn't willing, then they're justified trying to fulfill their desires with someone else because subtracting a crucial part of their relationship is something that can't go unaddressed.

Several men said they feel at a loss when they've made a commitment to be with one person, but it's become a sexual mismatch. That certainly was true for Nate, a twentysomething from Lexington, Kentucky. "In the beginning," he told me, "she gave me head, and then one day, all of a sudden, she said, 'Oh, I don't do that.' What do you mean you don't do that? You did it last month!"

Nate contined, "When I met my wife, oral sex was on

the menu. If I knew from the beginning that it wasn't on the menu, then I would have made a decision based on that—like, do I like her enough to go on without that? Probably yes, but getting it and then losing it made me feel like it was a bait and switch. But I was already invested in the relationship, we had been together for years, our lives were wrapped up together, so I'm not going to leave her over some head. But I really liked it when she gave me head, and I never got a straight answer about why she wasn't doing that anymore. So, I got a side piece who enjoyed doing it. If I cut my wife off from something that mattered to her, I wouldn't expect her to just sit there and accept it."

For a woman who is trying to figure out if her man is going to cheat on her someday, the personality traits and the mind-set were there already (or not) when the two of them started dating. Don't bother analyzing his feelings for you. In a sense, this is not about you. Instead, explore who he was and how he felt about women and relationships before you two met. Ask yourself the following:

- Does he regard himself highly? (Maybe too highly?)
- Is he extremely narcissistic?
- Does he need that high opinion validated repeatedly from others? A lot of cheaters have both high self-esteem and lots of insecurity, so that, on the one hand, they think they're great, but on the other hand, they need to hear that again and again.

- Is he overly nostalgic for the person he was in his twenties, when he was chasing women on the singles circuit? Or is he genuinely satisfied with having done that and is now truly ready to move on to the next chapter of life and monogamy?
- Is he attracted to danger, risk, and adrenaline?
- Does he lie frequently? Is he sneaky? Is he adept at concocting justifications for his lies?
- Does he think lying is okay depending on the circumstances?
- Is he good at hiding his feelings?
- Does he like feeling superior to other men and/or to women?

If he's overly self-absorbed, calculating, boyish, risk seeking, or apathetic toward your feelings, then he may already be open to the allure of Cheatingland. But some of those attributes are fun, and they may be hard to see clearly when you're in love with someone. Perhaps ask yourself about his friends. Many men may have one friend who is cheating on his wife, but if he has several? That's a red flag. Do his friends seem like they'd be willing to lie on his behalf?

Ultimately, if you're trying to see into the future and gauge how likely it is that he'll be unfaithful after you marry, the most important factor is this: Who taught him how to be a man, and what rules were involved in that? Was it his father, his uncle, his older brother, his mother? Once you identify his closest role models, explore *their* attitudes toward infidelity. Did they sleep around? Even if they didn't, is it possible that they encouraged your groom-to-be to sleep around? Of course, the most important person to pay attention to is his father. It may be hard to investigate Dad, but sniff around, use your intuition, and, if at all possible, ask questions. One of the surest ways to know if a man is going to end up cheating on his wife is to know the answer to this: Did his father cheat on his mother?

CHAPTER SIX

CHAPTER SIX

HOW HE GETS AWAY WITH IT

Every day in Cheatingland, people are mixing explosive chemicals and risking people's hearts and knowing that one wrong move could shatter lives. A cheater needs vigilance and constant circumspection because there are lots of lies to keep straight and feelings to manage. Many cheaters are constantly anxious, wondering, *Is today the day she'll find something?* He has to put in constant effort, like a criminal, always looking over his shoulder to see if the cops are on to him. The moment he lets down his guard could be the moment he gets caught and his life is ruined.

As Lucas from Austin cautioned, "Don't get comfortable,

no matter how easy it feels or how many times you got away. You still gotta work hard, like you just started. Look, this isn't for everybody, so if you're not going to go all out all the time and keep your tracks covered, then you don't need to be doing this at all. This ain't nothing to play with. You could be paying child support and alimony and living in another place real quick. It's not a game. If you're not willing to recognize that risk and know that you're gambling with some really serious stuff and that you have to take serious precautions and be on the lookout all the time, then don't even step into the arena."

Living a double life is a lot to handle. "It's really stressful living that secret life," said Lou from Houston. "Others may be better at it, but to me, it was hella stressful. Yes, it was exhilarating. Yes, there was a thrill. But it wore on me. I had to pay a heavy price to get that thrill. I like living a transparent life, where I can leave my phone out and not be scared. When I was screwing around, though, I was scared all the time. Scared my wife would see something on my phone or ask a question about where I was or "Who's this?" or something I couldn't answer. Scared my girlfriend would get mad and tell my wife what was going on. Scared that we would go out, and the wrong person would see us. Scared as hell that my kids would find out. I got so used to being scared all the time that I stopped totally noticing it; like, I normalized the fear because it was there all the time, which is completely crazy. Yeah, I was being secretive, and there was a thrill in that—there was fun in being all cloak-and-dagger—but the thrill came with a loud, buzzing stress in my ears all the time, a tightness in my shoulders all the time, a bug in my stomach all the time."

Larry from Chicago had a long-term girlfriend for many years during his marriage, and he ultimately found it to be corrosive. "It's very taxing in a sense that you're immersed in two situations at the same time, so you're constantly thinking about two women and making sure they're both happy; making sure your wife doesn't find out, and your side chick doesn't get too crazy, because you don't want to hurt anyone—that wasn't my intention. So, you're trying to navigate two relationships, and it can get really hard. I'm not trying to be corny, but there's not enough space in a day as a human being to have time to be present for two women."

Cheating takes so much work that multiple men described it as "a full-time job" because of how much thought, time, and effort go into it. Listen to Steve: "Men who are serious about this get really meticulous and pay attention to every little detail. You can't get sloppy. Every time you're with her, or every time your wife asks you an innocent question, is a chance to screw up. One mistake, and your whole life explodes. That's why you have to change the passcode to your phone every two weeks. You have to be careful when you two talk, and where you go, and all these things. This really is a full-time job."

Max, from Baltimore, seconded that, saying, "Your relationships are like another job. If you need to be to work at eight o'clock, then that's where the fuck you need to be at eight o'clock. If your wife says, 'Look, the bars close at two;

why can't you be here by two thirty?,' well then, you gotta
let your side chick know you need to be home by two thirty.
Know your time constraints. Cheating takes discipline. If
you're gonna cheat, you gotta be a very disciplined person."

Getting away with having a mistress, or more than one,
doesn't happen by accident. Men spend a lot of time thinking
about how to avoid detection and capture. "This is going to
come off like a really douchey thing to say," said Lou from
Houston. "But for me, it's always been that my wife is my
number one, in terms of I really care about this person, I love
this person, and the last thing I want to do is hurt this person.
That's why I needed to plan my screwing around carefully.
That's why I needed to make sure that I was protecting her.
I've got this voice in my mind constantly saying, *She can't
find out. She can never find out. Cover your tracks. Make sure
your times match up. Make sure your story is good.* 'Cause she's
not supposed to ever, *ever* find out. The moment she finds out,
it's not fun anymore. It's horrible."

The cheater's toolbox must be stocked with all sorts of
strategies and tactics for avoiding and escaping dangerous situations. A man who preferred not to give his name stressed,
"This is not for the faint hearted," adding, "I'm prematurely
gray because of it. It took a toll took on me."

· · ·

Now I'm going to open that toolbox and show you what's
inside that so you can see all the devices that men rely on to

get away with cheating. Some may see this as giving wives the playbook so that they know what's being used against them, but others will see this as giving future cheaters a road map—like handing out free instructions on how to make a bomb. Either way, many people will feel like this is dangerous information that's about to fall into the wrong hands. But here we go.

Cheaters practice in advance what they'll say if they get caught because they know the way they handle that moment could shape the rest of their lives. A famous womanizing jazz musician, who, though a bachelor, was actively juggling several women at once, said that if he ever got caught, he would deny it all, no matter what. Like an actor, he had his lines down pat, ready to deploy at any moment: "Oh, baby, she's just jealous of what we have! She's just trying to break up our happy home! Don't listen to her!" In one second flat, he could drop into character and nail the perfect "oh-so-sincere," imploring tone. This is a key component of the cheater's toolbox: the rehearsed lie. Always have it memorized so that it becomes the "truth," enabling you to override your brain's natural default to confess.

Mark from Las Vegas said, "Always have a good story. Like, I have a Wednesday men's business group. It's four guys that I have lunch with, and we talk about how to make more money. But sometimes, instead of actually meeting up with them, I go meet someone. If any questions ever come up about 'Where were you?' or 'What did you talk about?' or

'Who was there?' I'm ready. I tell her whatever we did at the *previous week*'s meeting. Being able to tell a lie with a straight face is the most important factor in pulling the wool over someone's eyes." In other words, before a liar can convince (lie to) his wife that he wasn't out cheating on her, he has to convince (lie to) himself.

Cheaters have to work hard to remember their stories because they usually have a lot of them to keep track of. Sam from New Orleans compares it to a Ponzi scheme. "You're building lie on top of lie, and it goes on and on until you've got so many branches in the tree of lies that you're just trying to figure out what's going to make it all break. You have to remember both *where you were* and *where you said you were* constantly and think in perspective of two women. It's a lot." Several cheaters told me they were shocked at how comfortable and proficient they became at lying all the time and keeping their fabrications straight. It's hard to catch someone in a lie when he's really good at it and so confident in his ability that he's not nervous about telling lies. And so, wives may have to look for other clues.

Many cheaters are scared to death that they'll be found out through social media and other apps because it's hard for most men to clean their phone often enough to eliminate every shred of incriminating evidence. However, wives don't really need to find a smoking gun on his phone to know what's going on. There's a simple question that can unmask him that most cheating men never plan for. A wife need only let her phone battery die, or pretend that her phone is dead, then turn to her husband and ask to use his phone. Without him saying a thing, his facial expression and body language will tell her all she needs to know. Matt, a married man with a girlfriend, re-marked, "Just the idea of handing my phone to my wife really scares me. Honestly, I try not to think about it. But there will be some day when she needs to look at something on Google and her phone is dead, and then there's some text or some pic-ture that I haven't erased that I can't let her see."

Nothing makes cheating easier than a man maintaining a sterling reputation with his spouse. If she believes him to be totally honest, he gets the benefit of the doubt if something seems potentially suspicious. Shawn from Maryland said, "I guess I kind of set a track record for myself in the first several years of our marriage, when I always was where I said I was and could always be believed. So, by the time I started going off the straight and narrow, she didn't have any reason to not believe me." Of course, building up a sparkling reputation and then risking it is like throwing your mortgage into the pot during poker. But people want to be able to trust their partner. It feels better to operate in an atmosphere of trust. Once a wife gets a feeling that something may be awry, though, once her faith is broken, she becomes seized by suspicion and its pals anxiety and dread. No one wants to be a detective in her own home, but it's hard to ignore those voices in the back of her mind once they start asking questions.

Carter, a thirtysomething from San Francisco, can attest

to this. "Once, I was doing the laundry, and I found a napkin on which my wife had scrawled the words 'I love Kevin.' I trust my wife completely and could not think of a moment when she could have been away from me to have had an affair with someone. So, finding that note did not rock my faith. But the question kicked around in my mind for days. What did that mean? I asked myself a slew of questions about how and when she could have conducted an affair, and I could not see it. I knew where she was all the time, and she usually responded to her phone pretty quickly, and I knew most of the people she was on the phone with. But that voice in my mind kept saying, *What does that mean?*

"Finally, I went to her and said, 'Look, I trust you completely, I'm sure this is nothing, but I found this note, and it won't leave my mind, so, like, what does this mean?' She explained without hesitation that she was talking with a girl-friend about her boyfriend—Kevin—and she was doodling as her friend was telling her what a good guy he was. I said okay, and I believed her because of the trust she had built up."

Once the questions start in your mind, however, you've got to ask. Why should you be alone with your suspicions? That said, most cheating husbands probably won't be forth-coming. They're not going to give up their secrets without leverage.

The foremost piece of advice cheaters offered to others is this: make sure your wife feels good about things. "When you're screwing around, the number one thing is you have to make sure home is happy," said Lucas from Austin. He's been married for more than a decade and cannot recall how many women he's slept with. "If home's not happy, then your wife is going to be on your ass, and it's not going to be as easy to cheat. If she's happy, she has no reason to suspect anything. Home has to be okay, or else this isn't going to work. Because if your wife is upset, she's going to be questioning everything. If she's not happy, when you're not home, you're giving her more time to think about all the reasons why she's upset. As long as you keep her happy and make her feel important and do nice shit for her, then you should be all right."

To that end, successful cheaters try to throw their wives off the scent by giving them everything they want, which is one of the ways that going to Cheatingland puts people through the looking glass. Christian, who's been with several women during his marriage, said, "At home, I was over-indulgent, I tried to overcompensate, I tried to do all the stuff I could think of to make her happy and give her no reason to question me." Sam from New Orleans said, "How did I keep it secret? The effort I put into seeing my girlfriend, I put the same amount of effort into my wife. It was like I had a clock or a meter running in my head, and if I spent an hour on my girl, I spent an hour on my wife. If I got flowers for my girl, I got 'em for my wife. If my girl got a gift, or my time, or whatever, I made sure my wife got that too. But there were plenty of things I did for my wife that I didn't do for my girl; I just had to make sure my wife never got less."

Disarming his wife with kindness makes it hard to know who's cheating, but it's still authentic for men who feel like the affair is not meant to be a rejection of their wife but an addendum to their lives. Christian said, "The main woman is always going to get the most attention, the most respect, the most everything. If she feels secure, then there's no reason for her questioning anything. I'm so serious about putting her first that there have been times during a sexual rendez-vous where I was midcoitus, my phone rang, and I stopped. I said, 'I'll be back in a moment,' and I stepped out on the bal-cony and had a conversation with my wife.

"It doesn't matter if it takes ten minutes or an hour," he continued. "The girl in my hotel room can be as mad as she wants, but I'll always put my wife before her. And I want her to know that I do. I've had women leave over me having a conversation like that with my main. Fine. But I've also had women say, 'Oh my gosh, that was so sweet. You're such a nice guy.' But I don't do it for them. I do it for my wife. And when they're all 'You're such a nice guy,' I'm thinking, *Yo, your men-tality is kinda fucked up right now. I still want to sleep with you, but this is not how you should be thinking.* But men do have to worry about what is going through their other woman's mind."

It is critical to also manage carefully the thoughts, expec-tations, and feelings of an affair partner. "I had to constantly make sure my side chick felt like I'm thinking about her," said Sam. "You can't just stop after you get the sex, 'cause if they feel like you just got over on them, that's when they're going to get messy and catty, and they're going to fuck your life up. If they feel used, then they're going to try to do something to blow your spot up, so you gotta make them feel seen and appreciated."

"You have to treat your affair partner with some importance," said Lucas. "You can't just make her feel like a booty call. You've got to continuously keep wooing her. Keep making her feel sexy, interesting, and fun. She wants you because having a married man is exciting for some women, but make her feel good. That's how you keep her on board and keep her from making things messy for you. You can't make her feel like the only time you're calling her is three o'clock in the morning. You've got to still treat her like a lady."

She likes the excitement and the danger of an affair too, but if the cheater makes her feel like she's being used, that he doesn't care about her at all, then she's going to get upset and may pour out her wounded heart to a third party. Maybe one of her friends. Or maybe his wife. So he's got to put in the effort to make her feel like he's not using her. But he can't get so close that she comes to believe that he loves her—or loves her enough to leave his wife—and ends up getting her heart broken. This delicate tap dance can become highly stressful, although it does have an upside. Matt from Raleigh said that cheating on his wife has forced him to be thoughtful about both of the women in his life. "You have to talk to each of your women," he said. "You have to listen to their feelings. You have to be on the phone with them; after you're done talking with one, you have to talk to the other one. There's so much to do when you have to take care of the emotions of two that it feels like a full-time job."

It is ironic that many men are unfaithful because they're unable to confide their emotional issues to their wives, yet when they're cheating, they have to be hyperaware of *two* women's emotional states, which probably demands more emotional work in the end. However, many men accomplish that while still remaining blind to their own feelings: the pain, the insecurity, the longing to be valued and cared for. All that's ignored because it's papered over by the ups and downs of being an adulterer.

One of the ways to keep affair partners happy is to be deeply honest. "I always say, 'Honesty first in my affairs,' " said Matt. My first affair partner told me, 'Hey, if you just let me know the situation, then I can deal with it. But when you take away my ability to understand what's going on and to really know what I'm dealing with, then I get furious.' She doesn't want to be fooled. So ever since then, whenever I meet someone, I'm up front and honest. I'm married, I love my wife, and I'm doing this 'cause I'm greedy. Through being honest, what I've found many times is that women will accept it and deal with it." If a man is clear about his availability and his feelings, and the other woman knows what she's getting, there's less of a chance that she'll end up hating him and feeling vengeful if things go sour.

Sam has been there. "My friends think it's funny and kind

of cool, but now it's normal for me to tell chicks what's up," he said. "I'll tell them exactly what's going on with me. I'll be up front about it: I'm married but I'm looking for some fun. Girls love that. If I need a new girl, they fall for that hook, line, and sinker. I've used that story multiple, multiple times, and I've never had it completely backfire on me.

"It's totally counterintuitive," he reflected. "They say they're looking for relationships, they say they don't want to be a number two, but they will because of their perception of masculinity. It might be Darwinian. Being with multiple people at the same exact time seems very masculine to them. I feel like I've got something figured out that other people don't. I swear to you that line has never not worked! It's way better to tell them what's up than to lure them in under false pretenses. Now, they're going to want an explanation, but if you give a sort of thoughtful explanation with a little emotion, it's not as goony-sounding as you think.

"I just slept with somebody last weekend who had been cheated on by her husband and is currently divorcing him," he went on. "She has no time for cheaters whatsoever. Probably my worst audience for it. Yet when I told her my real story and gave her my explanation, it didn't turn her off the way you would think it would. No, it was like chick crack. She loved it. I think she loved the honesty. She made fun of me about it a lot; she called me a slimeball. And she kept telling me how slimy I was right up to when she jumped in bed with me." Again, bear in mind that we are in Cheatingland, that bizzarro world where people have to remember to be honest with their affair partner while also remembering the lies they're telling their wives.

But having radical honesty with your paramours is part of the draw, men say. The release that comes with being able to say anything and everything feels liberating. Why would a man feel more free to share his deepest emotions with a mistress than with his own wife? Because there's little to lose. Where he might fear losing his wife if his emotional honesty puts her off in some way, he doesn't fear getting dumped by an affair partner. For starters, she's replaceable. Besides, being honest feels good, and it helps bond the two more quickly.

However, there's a caveat to this: according to some of my interview subjects, as much as a man may enjoy sharing secrets with affair partners, they advise not disclosing personal, identifying details, such as his home address or where he works. Yes, welcome to yet another weird contradiction of Cheatingland, a place where a man can share the deepest secrets he wouldn't tell anyone but not the basic facts he'd discuss in small talk with strangers because what happens if one day she gets mad? What if she goes to the man's house? Or his office? Cheaters must try to keep things placid and peaceful no matter what.

Mike from St. Louis has cheated several times. "When I get into an argument with my girlfriends, I'm careful," he said. "I'm never gonna call you out. I'm never gonna curse you. I'm never gonna call you no bitch, no ho. I got no disrespect for you. That goes a long way toward making sure the end of the relationship is cool. The worst thing I'll say is, 'Okay, I'm not messing with you no more.'" The last thing a cheater wants is to destroy his girlfriend's feelings and leave her angry, hurt, and alone with time to figure out how to retaliate. There's nothing more dangerous than a vengeful ex-girlfriend. She has secrets that he doesn't want his wife, or his family, or his community to know. As long as she feels respected and that she hasn't been deceived, he can probably trust her to be quiet. But if they have a crazy fight, she could morph into a supervillain with a weapon that could decimate him, and he can't do anything to stop her.

This power is why cheaters have to be extremely careful about who they pick to sleep with. This is critical to getting away with it. If you were going to rob a bank, you'd think long and hard about which accomplice to bring along. One of the primary factors in your decision would be whether you think a given person would stay silent if caught. Who would not snitch? This same sort of thinking goes into choosing an affair partner: the man has to know that he can trust her because an ex-girlfriend—or even a girlfriend—could blackmail him at any time.

Steve from the Midwest said, "I don't want to let somebody into my inner sanctum of kinks and do crazy things with them that I don't want anyone to hear about and then have her start intimating that if I leave her, she might get upset and tell someone that we were together and use the weird stuff I like to embarrass me. Look, I don't want her mentioning my wife at all. If she does, that's a major red flag. If she talks about my wife, I have to escape very quickly, but carefully—because she's holding very dangerous secrets, and she's signaling that she's willing to use them. The time she's most likely to divulge your trash is when you're trying to leave her or right after you've left her.

"On a couple of occasions, I've opened myself up to people who turned out to be disastrous, crazy people, and it almost cost me my whole shebang. I mean, she went crazy and was calling the house! I survived those moments, and, nowadays, I am much more trepidatious about letting myself be with someone who gives off any sense that they can come back and hurt me. You have to go through some tests. You have to provide some emotional collateral. I have to know what you're capable of. I have to know you'll be on my side forever."

Matt: "It's all about recruitment. If you recruit the right people, you don't have a whole lot to worry about."

Randy: "Be exceedingly careful who you get involved with. And if you're going to go down this road, then understand what it is you want out of the situation and what your expectations are, so that way there's no misunderstandings later on. If they're even thinking about looking for a new relationship, let them know, 'Let's not do this anymore.' If they want you to leave your wife, you should run. The second that comes up, you know that's not going to end well."

As for picking the "right" woman to cheat with, that can

mean many things. For example, Randy, along with many other of the men I talked to, said it makes a lot of sense to choose someone who lives in another city, thus putting literal as well as figurative distance between her and the cheater's everyday world. "I'm very big on not being with people who have any sort of connection to my real life," he said. "You have to be wary. If this person can identify you, can easily come to your house or your job, that's nerve-wracking. You're giving them too much power. You have to be absolutely certain that they can't destroy your life. With that in mind, you must pick and choose carefully. My advice is don't get involved with people you work with and absolutely avoid everyone who knows your wife. My God, if you're gonna do that, why don't you just juggle grenades with one hand?"

One issue that was hotly debated was whether it is safer to pursue married or single women. According to Randy, "One of my rules is that I only cheat with married women. You never want to cheat with someone who doesn't have as much to lose as you do. I prefer married women because they're putting their lives on the line just like you are. Life is way simpler when they're not looking at you as a potential next husband, and they just want to sneak off from their life and have fun and then go home, and they know they're not supposed to fall in love." Many cheaters said that if you have a partner who has a lot at stake, they'll fight just as hard as you to keep things quiet, even after it all ends—as long as you both remain clear on where things are going.

"When I started seeing my high school ex-girlfriend," Randy said, "we went into it with the expectation that I wasn't going to change her marriage, and she wasn't going to change my marriage. Then she started to get what they call 'the feels.' I had the feels too, but I was under control. But she had the feels to the point where she was really thinking about leaving her husband and wanting me to leave my wife. I was not prepared for that. It created a huge mess."

Of course, the challenge when it comes to cheating with a married woman is that she has a husband. And if he ever finds out what's happening, that's often a gigantic problem. People have been murdered for sleeping with other men's wives. Scott from Dallas said, "When you're talking about somebody's wife, you're talking about emotions getting out of hand. I'm not trying to get killed over no woman. And I came close! I left my house and was walking down the street when this man said, 'Hey, is your name Scott?'

"I was, like, 'Yeah, that's me,' and I extended my hand. Next thing I know, I got knocked out. He hit me with a pair of brass knuckles! He knocked me out in the middle of the street. I'm coming to, and I hear a car coming toward me, and I'm saying, 'Oh my God, this dude is about to run me over and kill me!' The car pulls up next to me, tires screech, and he says, 'Leave my fucking wife alone, motherfucker!' Then he takes off down the street. After that, I said to myself, *No more married women. Ever!*"

Scott was lucky. Mark had a much closer brush with

death. "He caught us at the motel and came up to the room with a gun," he said. "He threatened her, threatened me. I was like, 'Yo, listen, your problem is with her, not with me. I don't even know you. I'm leaving.' Dude pointed the gun at me, so I said, 'Look, if you gonna shoot, then shoot, but if you do, you're gonna spend the rest of your life in prison, so what's up? You gonna squeeze it or what?' I stood there for a few seconds, and he stood there pointing it at me and breathing all hard, and I said, 'You ain't squeezing that. I'm out of here.' I walked out and left her there.

"About a year later, I saw her out somewhere, and she came running over, like, 'I don't believe you left me!' I was, like, 'He had a gun! What was I supposed to do? Fight for your honor? You weren't even my chick!'"

Steve laid out the rules for when you're confronted by an angry partner. "Here's what you do: don't admit anything to the husband! You don't owe him an admission. You acknowledge that he's angry. You apologize for him being angry. You say that you've extricated yourself from the situation, and you're never going to contact his wife again. Just defuse the situation."

Randy said much the same: "If you're confronted by the spouse, don't admit to anything. Certainly don't admit to anything in writing. End the conversation as quickly and as carefully as possible." An angry, cuckolded husband is looking to scare off a cheater, but he's also looking for revenge. He may be so enraged that he could hurt or kill. He may feel he needs to reassert his manhood—a cheater basically takes that away from him by sleeping with his wife—so the way to defuse things is by being humble and acquiescing to his dominance. Randy said, "If he feels like he's lost his manhood, and he's trying to get it back by making you bitch up, then you might have to do that. It could save your life. That's not the time to show him how tough you are. As soon as you can get away, do that. People really do get killed in moments like that. You gotta get out."

All of that is why many men said they prefer an affair partner who's not married. Also, with single women, scheduling time to be together is easier because her calendar is not dotted with familial obligations. Of course, having an affair partner who's single can be challenging. Owen said, "People who are single have a lot of time to think about why you're not there. Girls who are single are a headache. I would never recommend that. If you're dealing with somebody who's got to go home and watch their children and whatever, they don't have time to pine over why you aren't there. And they've got a lot to lose—they don't want to lose their kids. So, they want to have fun and then be quiet. That's perfect. I want someone who's gonna get with me, take that little vacation from life, then get back to life, and not worry about us until the next time we meet up." People who are single are more likely to fall in love and expect a cheater to leave home for them, which can lead to a hellish situation.

Whichever sort of affair partner he chooses, most men

said it was paramount to always keep in mind that their wife is their primary woman, and one way of showing that is to never talk badly about their wife to their girlfriend. The hierarchy must always stay clear. Confiding in the girlfriend about what's wrong with the cheater's marriage is disrespectful and gives the affair partner extreme power and may give her hope that a separation or divorce is on the horizon. If she were ever to repeat what the cheater said about his wife to her, it would cut her deeply in many ways at once. Randy offered some advice for the other woman: "If someone is dissing his spouse to you, then you should run for the hills. Because if he's going to shit on her, then you have no idea what he's going to say about you down the road." Cheaters say it's best for affair partners to not talk about their wives at all—ideally, they want a separation of church and state. What's best is an affair that's an oasis away from his real life, that doesn't even mention his real life. When his girlfriend is talking about his wife, that means that she's thinking about her—and that can be dangerous.

Nathan, the actor from Cleveland, said, "If the chick that you're cheating with wants to talk a lot about your main, and she keeps bringing that up, cut 'em off because that's when it's getting to the point to where things are going in the wrong direction and something out of the ordinary might happen. The side chick should be focusing on you and the two of you. If your main is in her mind, pull the rip cord and get the hell out of there."

. . .

Another tactic that some cheaters use to throw off the scent is taking both their wives and their girlfriends to the same restaurants and the same movies, and so on, thus making it easier to keep the memories straight and lessen the potential of saying the wrong thing. Several felt that minimizing the number of places all of you go is the simplest path. Jackson, a thirtysomething living in LA, said, "I always take my girlfriend to do the same sort of stuff me and my wife did together. So, you're in one section of a restaurant on a Wednesday night and a different section on a Thursday night. I had to see *Dumb and Dumber* twice. I saw all these different movies twice because I had to see the same thing with my wife and my girlfriend. Which is like a bad movie plot by itself. You don't know how much acting I had to do when I went to a bad movie for the second time, and I had to laugh at a dumb joke I'd already seen but had to make it seem like I didn't know the laugh was coming. It was a lot."

Sam from New Orleans said, "One of my friends who taught me a lot of the ropes of all this, he said he would do stuff like take all the women he was seeing to the same restaurant. Then he would be less likely to screw up his conversation. So, yeah, he went to Olive Garden on Wednesday with his wife and on Friday with his mistress, so if he ever talked about going to Olive Garden, there were no questions, like, 'When did you go to Olive Garden?'"

Not everyone is sharp enough to pull this off, including Sam, who said, "I could never be that meticulous. He subscribes to the opposite school of thought, which is to carry on two entirely separate relationships. "I had a full double life—one track with my wife and one with my side girl—and each one was totally different," he explained. "I was pretty much able to compartmentalize everything, but it's almost impossible. It takes up almost all of your brain bandwidth. There wasn't that much I could think about beyond what was happening on each side of my life and making sure I never said the wrong thing to anyone." Some of the men I interviewed spoke of taking their wife to, say, foreign movies and nice restaurants, while bringing their other woman to dingy motels and dive bars. That sort of bifurcation helps cheaters keep the two situations totally distinct in their minds.

Men in this camp said it was important to take their affair partner to places that are outside their usual circle of activity, thus giving them a layer of protection if someone sees them. Lou from Houston said, "When I meet my girls out, I take 'em to the gay part of town. If we're in a gay bar a few towns over and you see me, I bet you won't say anything because you probably didn't want anyone to see you there. Just like me. So we're cool."

Whether a cheater is taking his women to the same places or different ones, there are all sorts of ways he can get caught. Many men said they're too nervous to sit at a table when they're on dates, so they always sit at the bar. Matt, who's married and has been in an ongoing affair for the last six years, said, "We sit at the bar so that, hypothetically, if somebody looks at us and has a question about what's going on, I'm just having a drink with a friend at the bar. We don't go to the table in the corner. That's too public. You have to plant plausible deniability. You also have to know your escape route out of the place in case the wrong person walks in. If you're at the bar, it's way easier to dip out in a flash." However, to the other woman, having to sit at the bar instead of at a table may seem like a sign of disrespect as if she's not good enough for a table.

When the cheater pays the bill, there's a chance of leaving behind evidence that can sink him. If he doesn't pay cash, there's a record on his credit card, but using cards or a mobile payment service such as Apple Pay leaves a clear record of where you were. Many cards have websites so simple that a child can navigate them. To be honest, many Zoomer kids are better at anything online than their Gen Xer parents, but the point is that these sites are extremely incriminating. If a husband buys something at a store his wife doesn't recognize—or is suddenly using his ATM a lot more—these are clear signs that something may be going on. Cards are critical for navigating the modern world, as most decent hotels don't take cash, and neither does Uber or Lyft. If a cheater travels by Uber to or from a date, he is putting a record of exactly where he was, and when, on his phone as well as a notice on his card. Cards make it easy for wives to catch cheaters. Any-

time he puts a large amount on his card, it's very conspicu-
ous—big numbers scream out, "Dinner for two!"

Matt offered some expert advice: "When you go out
with your girlfriend, go dutch if possible. That helps keep
it quiet. If you can find somebody that's okay with footing
the bill, that's good. You don't want to accumulate all these
suspiciously high restaurant bills. Not too long ago, I went
out with a girl, and we both had a couple of drinks, and the
tab came to eighty dollars. If you try to say you spent that
by yourself, that's a lot to drink on your own. That's hard
to explain. 'You drank that with a buddy? Why'd you pay
instead of him?' That's a lot of questions to answer, and the
more questions, the more likely you'll screw up. If you tell
the bartender to split it down the middle, forty bucks at a bar
isn't hard to explain. But eighty dollars says that someone
else was there."

Modern technology creates all sorts of virtual bread-
crumbs that make it easy to figure out where someone was
at any given time. Some people combat all of this by getting
a credit card that their spouse knows nothing about. But
even then he's got to hide the bills and whatever other no-
tices come from the company, because once a wife realizes
that he's got a card he didn't tell her about, she's filled with
questions about what life is being funded through that card.
And if there's just dinner and hotel and La Perla and Manolo
Blahnik charges on it, she can see what's going on.

Mike, who lives in San Antonio, said, "At one point, I had

a secret, separate bank account. I had my check from my job direct deposited, and a percentage of that check went to a separate account that I was able to use without anybody asking what the money was for or where it was going. It was at a whole different bank. I felt like I was legitimately living two separate lives." That sort of monetary subterfuge is necessary but also vulnerable to a wife's interrogation.

Experienced cheaters know they must pay close attention to their online footprint, especially what goes on their phone. "The cell phone is absolutely the biggest problem," Sam from New Orleans said.

Lots of the men in my study talked about getting burner email accounts and cell phones that have a short shelf life, as well as apps that help cloak connections. Several had their phones encrypted so that messages remain private.

"Don't use your phone for the relationship," Randy said. "It's way too easy to get caught through your phone." Communicating through texts is so dangerous that men need apps to help cover their digital tracks. Peter said, "I had a little secret text messaging app, and whenever I went home, I would delete the app, and then I'd go on the app store and search a whole bunch of stuff so my recent finds list would not show that text message app. Crazy, but I had to be certain." He also had an app that gave him an excuse to get away from a girlfriend quickly. "The app that would call my phone and make it look like my mom was calling me. I'd pick up and be, like, 'Alright, Mom, I'll be over in a little bit.'"

Too much communication with an affair partner can leave cheaters far too vulnerable and make them easier to catch. Men say they have to establish clear boundaries regarding times when it's acceptable to text or call because having a wide-open channel is like playing with fire. "I don't want no good-morning text, no good-night text," Nathan, the actor, said, "Don't send me none of that shit. We talk at specific times, not all day long."

Social media has made it easier to meet and connect with new people who are outside of a person's normal social circle. The fewer people the two cheaters know in common, the easier it is to keep the affair a secret. Of course, that increased connectivity works in many ways—social media means that anyone can contact anyone, including a girlfriend contacting a wife, or a concerned friend reaching out to a wife, or a wife reaching out to a strange name she sees on her husband's phone.

A cell phone is a record of almost everything its owner has done, said, and thought about deeply. In moments, anyone can see who someone texted or called, what he Googled, where he went—for instance, if he drives to meet someone and uses Waze or Google Maps or some other GPS tracker, it won't take much work to decipher exactly where he's been, so he might as well just keep a diary and hand it to his wife. For most people who get caught, what gives them away is their phone. Wives who want to know what's really going on can figure it out through his phone. There's often some little piece of the affair left lingering on the phone: the cute text that didn't get deleted, the unfamiliar location in the Maps app, the phone number that wasn't erased. All sorts of things that can raise questions. The phone is like a tech version of the bloody footprints that lead cops from the crime scene to the killer.

According to Matt, "You have to clean your phone out every day. A friend of mine got caught up when a girlfriend sent him some pictures, and he kept them, and his wife went in his phone and found them. She wasn't even looking for anything. She just stumbled on them. These aren't the sort of pictures you can explain away. Why he had sexy pictures on his phone, I do not know—that's a huge no-no—but he did. You've got to delete everything. Hold it in your memory, and that's it."

Men who like holding on to salacious pictures or X-rated texts or crazy voice mails are just clinging to evidence that will get them caught. Christian said, "You've got to cover your tracks. Tell me why dudes get caught with text messages on their phone? Why the fuck are you keeping those text messages? They're meant to be disposable. Do you want to go back and read them? Once you get the text, delete it."

There are so many tracks to cover and so many things to worry about. A thirtysomething from North Carolina who wouldn't give his name said, "The biggest help is I have a Google voice number, so no chick I've ever been with actually has a number to a cell phone that would ring when I'm beside my wife. Do not use the same number that you use to talk to your wife because eventually that's gonna come back and bite you in the ass. Technology will screw you over! You can delete your Facebook messages, but, I swear to God, a female can get on there and find them. You can get caught so many ways because technology is constantly monitoring where you are. So, you have to do a lot of careful planning on where you're going to do this and when and how."

Some guys said they find Google products frightening because of the level of automatic integration between them: for example, if a man is on his phone in one city, trying to catch a flight and writing a note in his calendar about who he'll call when he gets to the hotel, a contact card might pop up on his computer at home—and maybe his wife is there to see it. Or he could be searching for restaurants to hit up, and it'll trigger something on a Chrome browser at home.

Scott from Dallas said, "If you're going to cheat, you should get off the grid entirely. Turn off your phone so it doesn't track your location. Turn all notifications off. Be careful what addresses you plug in. Be careful about calling someone from a phone that you're not going to throw away. Memorize her number so it doesn't have to live in your phone. And don't say anything at all on social media. Just stay off of Facebook. Stay off of Instagram. So many marriages have been broken up because of fucking social media. You can get away with Twitter, but all these other ones? No way. You cannot cheat nowadays and be on social media. You are going to get caught." Charlie said, "Social media makes it way too easy for people to track you down. I can find virtually anyone who's online. It's really scary."

In a world where anyone can reach out to anyone at any time, and everyone has a camera, and devices memorialize where people have been, cheating men have so much to fear—so many areas of vulnerability. It's easy for his name or his picture to pop up on anyone's radar. One man said he almost got caught when a friend of a friend of his wife's saw him at dinner with another woman. He avoided being outed only because the friend of the friend thought the other woman was his wife, so she didn't take a photo. She just texted the cheater's wife to say that she had seen her and her husband at the such-and-such restaurant, and they looked cute together. When the wife confronted her husband, demanding to know who he was with, he had a lie prepared—"It was just someone from work"—and she let it go. His marriage was saved only because he hadn't been photographed; the body language surely would have given away that it was more than a meet-up between colleagues.

Yes, photos can be deadly. Many men recommended never taking pictures with their affair partners. Andrew, who has had several affairs, said, "If you get tagged in a picture, and the other girl is in that picture, you're screwed. You're dead in the water. Remember that scene in *The Godfather* where they're smashing cameras at the wedding? They were like, 'No pictures!' And I'm like, 'No tagging me in anything!'" In this era of the virtual surveillance state, cameras are ubiquitous, our cellphones are pinging a tower every few seconds, and it feels nearly impossible to have a secret life or even a private moment that will never be uncovered, which is why cheaters can be caught by wives who know where to look.

If a husband is following his affair partner on social media, that makes it easier for a wife to find her if she starts digging around. Then again, the married cheater who's posting cute pictures of his family on social media is essentially flaunting those pics right in his mistress's face, which spoils the fantasy aspect of Cheatingland and underscores everything that's at risk because of the affair. Lauren, who's been married for more than a decade, has a married boyfriend. She used to follow him on social. "We were Facebook friends for a while," she said, "but that's not happening anymore. I got to feeling like, 'I really don't need to see your happy family pictures.' Then you find yourself obsessing over them, which is really not good. We're no longer Facebook friends, and I prefer feeling cut off from that part of his life. I know he has a wife and kids; I just don't need to see them."

One thing many men do is keep their lovers on their phone under fake names, especially male names, to add a layer of security just in case a wife sees something that could be suspicious. Scott said, "When my girl calls, it comes up as 'Kenny.' That's really slimy, and if my wife ever figured out that Kenny was a woman, it would be instant game over. But she hasn't, and that got me through two years of screwing around."

Finding time to have a tryst is a whole challenge in itself. When do people meet and not raise suspicions? Rendezvousing during the day lessens the potential of being detected—absences during the workday are less likely to arouse suspicion at home. One of my subjects had a secret apartment a few blocks from his office. He would leave work a little early and meet his girlfriend there around four or five, have fun, and be home by six or seven, showered, happy, and ready for dinner with his wife and kids, with no one the wiser. One woman I interviewed said she had her affair partner come visit her at home around lunchtime, while her husband was at work. Lou from Houston said, "It's all about finding the right hours of the day and finding the right people who are willing to play by those rules. There ain't no hanging out on Saturday night at one o'clock in the morning. We'll connect at happy hour, do our thing, and be wrapped up by seven. There's just a real tight window of plausible opportunity—a window of time where your hangouts are believably innocent. If you can't meet in that window of innocence, then it just doesn't happen."

A cheater may find it easier to schedule dates if he has a job that doesn't have a set daily schedule. Lucas from Austin said, "In my work, my hours can change at any time, and my wife knows that. So I can say to her at any time, 'Hey, I'm working overnight tonight,' and she'll accept it, and after she's gone to sleep, I come home happy. Because my schedule keeps changing, she can't keep track of my hours, so she doesn't know where I'm supposed to be at any given time. Which is perfect."

One man drives for Uber as a side hustle, giving him a lot of flexibility for seeing his girlfriend. "Sometimes I say I'm gonna go out and drive," he said, "but I actually go meet somebody and hook up with her."

Men who travel for work have it very easy making time for other women. On any work trip, there's downtime, the chance to meet women, and an empty bed where he can take them. Cheating on the road requires less trickery, and if he's habitually in another city, it's not hard to build relationships. Traveling is so valuable at facilitating infidelity that some men invent fictional work trips, like Sam from New Orleans.

"I do a lotta fake trips," he said. "I love saying, 'I'm going down to Mexico with my buddies,' but I'm actually going to Mexico with her. I travel two to three weeks a month, so it's totally believable." The cheater just has to keep his lies straight. Sam said, "Yeah, you have to remember both where you said you were going to be and where you actually were at any given time, and where those two diverge, so that you don't make a mistake. But after a while it starts to become rote. You see your life in two different paths: what you did and what you were supposed to have done, and you talk only about what you were supposed to be doing. Over time I became amazing at it. I never missed a beat."

Jake from Memphis, said, "I'm always flying out on Monday and coming back home on Thursday, week after week, and I have so many frequent-flyer miles and a corporate card, so I can hide things. One time I didn't have a project for six weeks, but the whole time I was flying out on Monday and flying back home Thursday. Instead of work, I was in Puerto Rico with this girl. Sometimes I said I was flying out, and I packed a bag and left and drove to her place on the other side of town and stayed there for a few days. But I was maintaining my routine, so my wife didn't notice."

Some men are ninja silent about what they're doing on the side and never talk about it. Others are *dying* to talk about it, especially Peacocks. Sometimes sharing the story—and showing off their trophies—is part of the ego boost. Some men want others to know that they have the cojones to go out and get extra. But the more people who know a secret, the less likely it can be kept. "I didn't tell anyone," Greg from Baltimore said. "Well, eventually I told one person, and that was it. I didn't tell anyone else. I was very secretive. If it was one of the rare times when me and my affair partner were out in public together, we made sure we were somewhere where there would be no one else we knew. I was always afraid of being spotted."

Cheaters who talk about their affair are risking everything. "Bragging is the kiss of death," Jackson said. "You're going to puff your chest out and want to tell people what you did. Just like you want to tell people you scored twenty points in that pickup game in the park. You want people to know you're the man. Don't do it." But human beings love to tell stories, especially if they happen to be the star. The only place to talk about it safely is to participate in an online forum about adultery. Randy, who's been married twenty years and is currently involved with several other women, said, "Sometimes you need to talk about the joy that you're having or ask a question when you're in a sticky situation. That's why things like a Facebook adultery group are so important because you need to share sometimes."

Cheaters' secrets often escape through the mouth, but they also manifest physically. How? One way is that a man who has been sleeping with another women, or more, may betray his betrayal when he's making love to his wife. Several men talked about the challenge of being with someone else and then being the same sexually as he always was with his wife. Many couples have a unique chemistry when dancing between the sheets, and if he's having sex with someone else, he may have developed some different habits. When he has sex with his wife, if he pulls off brand-new moves that she has never seen after years of marriage—even if it's just a minor deviation from the usual—she might take notice: *Uh, he's never done that before. I wonder why he's doing that now . . .* ? And from there, it's not much of a leap to wondering if her husband isn't getting practice elsewhere.

When he's with another woman, her scent can get imprinted on his body in a way that can be hard to get off. Now, a woman's sense of smell is generally more sensitive than a man's—if he's not careful, he may not even notice his romantic partner's scent on him, and that will totally give him away. Men's poor sense of smell compared with women's is a big disadvantage that a cheater has to compensate for carefully. Many men tell their affair partners to not wear perfume and also to go easy on the lipstick. Wives can smell a tiny bit of someone else's fragrance or notice a little smidge of a lipstick color that's not hers. As clichéd as they are, those little things will get a cheater caught.

"I'll hit the gym before I go home," said Christian from Miami. "I'll spend an hour there getting in a really good workout. Then I shower at the gym just to make sure the smell is gone." But if he's a man who doesn't normally come home freshly showered or doesn't usually jump in the shower as soon as he gets home, once he starts doing that, it's a red flag. If his routine changes in some significant way, it could be a sign that he's responding to his life having changed in some way. When cheaters get into a new entanglement, their life *has* changed, but they must avoid making changes to their routine at home so as not to raise their wives' suspicions. Kevin, the man who, as a child, had been an eyewitness to his father's philandering, said, "I was careful to never change up my routine. I don't think I really had to keep it a secret because I didn't do anything out of the norm."

Ironically, for some unfaithful husbands, keeping it all a secret means entangling other people in their web. If he's a Peacock, he's going to be trafficking in so many lies that he may need a confederate who can sometimes "confirm" that he was where he said he was (even though, in reality, he wasn't). If he's a Completer, he may need a reasonable excuse to have time to see his other woman. A Dead Bedroomer may need someone to run interference for him while he hangs out with his special friend during or after work.

Cheating is a game of stealth conducted in the shadows under false pretenses that are built on a foundation of lies. Many people have one or two close friends who are willing to bury a body for them. Matt said, "One of my closest friends says there has to be honor among thieves. There will be one person who you should clue in—someone who knows your wife and is willing take a bullet for you from time to time." A woman who declined to give her name said, "You need allies in your lies. You gotta have backup a little bit. People who are sworn to secrecy. People who will be your alibi if you need that, and you know they will never tell no matter what."

Once he engages his confederates, his life is in their hands. They can't back out or screw up if his wife starts asking questions. Tom said, "If I say, 'Hey, babe, I'm going out with some guy to have drinks,' and that guy forgets and posts something on Instagram that doesn't fit my story, and my wife sees it, then I'm dead in the water. If you say you're gonna be my alibi, it takes a lot of awareness. It's easy to forget and post the wrong thing and unwittingly give up the ghost and let her see that I'm lying." Confederates have to stay focused on the cheater's lies and make sure they don't violate his trust, which is tricky, so he can't ask so much of them that it screws up their lives.

Carter: "So, my married homeboy texts me and says, 'Hey, I'm throwing a birthday party for my girlfriend, and you gotta come 'cause there's only, like, eight people who know about her, and I'm trying to make it really nice, so I really need you to be there.' Now, this is a good friend who's done a lot of nice things for me, so I can't just say no. He's calling in a favor, and he's way ahead in the favor trade, and I take that seriously. But this favor puts me in a really crappy spot: my wife knows this guy, she loves the guy, and she loves parties, so if I say to my wife that I'm going to a party that he's throwing, she'll say, 'Oh, great, I'll go with you!' But she didn't know he was having an affair, and she sees his wife twice a week at the kids' soccer practice. If she knew that he was fooling around, it would put her in a bind: she'd have to look his wife in the face while holding on to a secret that she was never meant to know. She didn't promise to keep a secret, and it could be really painful and guilt inducing for her to do so. What if she turns around and says, 'I can't keep lying to this woman; it makes me feel like an asshole'? What then? But if I tell her she can't come to the party, she'll be, like, 'What are you talking about? What's going on?' She'll be looking at me, like, Why are you lying to me?

"So, I'm hemming and hawing about what to do, and he keeps texting me and pushing me to RSVP. I'm thinking,

Am I supposed to lie to my wife about where I'm going so that *I can protect your lie?* That could get me in a lot of trouble. Why is his lying becoming an issue in my marriage? Like, it's about to ruin my good name with my wife. I don't want to lie to my wife and create a problem for me. But I don't want to lie to him and be a bad friend.

"I'm going back and forth about what to do, and then, lucky me, a business trip fell into my lap that put me out of town on the day of his party. Suddenly I can't go. Bullet dodged, crisis averted. I don't have to figure out how to get my wife out of going, I don't have to lie to anyone. Everything's cool. I can finally exhale.

"And then, totally out of nowhere—I hadn't even mentioned this guy to my wife in weeks because I was all stressed about this situation—I'm sitting at the table, not talking, and my wife just looks at me and says, 'Is he having an affair?' She had never said anything like that about any of my friends. I don't even know why she said that or what made her think of him at that moment—I hadn't told her anything about him or my dilemma—but after going through all of that and being so confused because I was determined to not lie to her, I just said, 'Yeah, he is.' I didn't want to tell her because I didn't want to burden her and I didn't want to betray his confidence, but I wasn't going to lie to her. She said, 'I knew it,' And she walked off and never said anything else about it."

Guys who are truly clever can turn their affair partner into their own confederate by normalizing her presence in his life so that they have a girlfriend who's basically hiding in plain sight. That way, he doesn't have to be secretive all the time. In Randy's words, "If you make it so that you have a legit reason to actually be with that person—like, for work or school or something so that your interacting with them is understandable—then you're home free. I always try to normalize it so there's no question about 'Why are you texting so-and-so at eleven o'clock at night?' 'Oh, we're working on this thing together.'"

One of my interview subjects told me about a man who took the effort to normalize his relationship pretty far. He lived in Atlanta with his wife, while his girlfriend resided in Detroit. They decided that they would begin meeting periodically in DC under the guise of working on establishing a prisoners' rights organization that would be headquartered there. The man told his wife all about the organization he'd cofounded, and from that point on, whenever he said he had to travel to DC for a meeting, she didn't think anything of it. This arrangement carried on for several months without a hitch until he mentioned his fake prisoners' right organization in front of his wife's father, who was a retired judge who cared deeply about prison reform. Dad-in-law asked if he could go to DC with him to witness a board meeting of his new group in action. Sure, the man said. He couldn't say no to his father-in-law. But how could he show him an organization that didn't exist?

Flash cut to a fancy restaurant in DC and four people

happily eating dinner: The cheater, his father in law, and two people who said they were members of the executive board. They were the man's girlfriend and the friend who told me this story. The dinner table conversation leaned heavily on plans for an upcoming fundraiser. Pure fiction. Dad did his best to follow their conversation, but at eighty, he was unable to see the wool they were pulling down over his eyes.

The lengths some people go to keep it all quiet are amazing.

CHAPTER SEVEN

WHEN CHEATING GOES WRONG

Cheating is incredibly dangerous. If it is Russian Roulette, then it's a version where there is more than just one bullet in the chamber, *and* the barrel is pointing at several heads at once. People who get caught can find themselves in a world of pain where they can lose their marriage, their family, their money, their mind, their body, their spirit—everything is at risk. The safest thing is not to cheat in the first place.

That's the road most men take, but warning adulterers not to fool around on their wives because it's dangerous is a losing proposition. In fact, for many men, the danger is part of the fun. The stress, the challenge, the chaos—all of it adds an adrenaline rush that's akin to skydiving, and some people just can't hold themselves back. Which is why it can become like an addiction.

Jamie from Atlanta said, "It's like the pussy is calling my name and saying, 'Come fill me up again!' I can't say no! I'm obsessed." As with any addiction, it's possible for things to spiral out of control, and that's when lives can get destroyed, like in Darren's case.

"Once, I came back from a trip," he said, "and as soon as I walked in the house, I realized I still had a little condom box in my pocket. I was like, 'What the fuck is this doing in my pocket? I need to get rid of this!' So, when my wife went in the other room, I stashed it in the bottom of a garbage can. I reached in through all the slop and the goop and the mess and made sure that box was all the way on the bottom of the bag. *No one's going to see that*, I thought. *Okay, cool, problem solved*.

"Later that evening, my wife comes to bed and taps me on the shoulder. I mumbled, 'Hey, yeah, what's up?' She says, "Oh, you're awake. Okay, I have a question for you: Why is there an empty condom box in the garbage?'

"I said, 'I don't know what you're talking about. They're not from me. I don't know. How'd you find it? What are you talking about?' She said, 'Yeah, I was taking out the trash, and the bag busted, and this box was the first thing that came out, so you must've put it at the bottom because it's underneath what I had for dinner last night.' I went through all the trouble to put it at the bottom of the trash, and the bag breaks, and *that's* the first thing to pop out! We had a very long talk—and we almost got divorced—but I talked my way out of that, somehow."

A few other men had far grimmer stories to tell. Adulterers who get caught may find themselves bankrupted, or they may lose visiting rights to their children—or they could even be killed by, say, a mistress's jealous boyfriend or by an enraged wife. Cheaters are gambling with their lives and assuming they won't get caught. True, most don't, but when they do, things can get crazy. Here's a series of stories about what happened after people got caught. Stories of worlds collapsing. Plenty of cheaters who get caught talk it out with their spouse, maybe with a therapist too, and work things out. We'll look more closely at how they do that in the next chapter. But for some people, things can turn catastrophic. Horror stories can occur. Lives can be changed for the worst. Meet several people who will regret cheating forever.

. . .

Larry from Chicago said his life changed forever after he got caught. His kids' lives, too. After he moved to a new city and picked up some clients one of them, a married woman who was several years older than him, started showing him around town.

During their trips driving around and lunching together, she began talking about the difficulties in her marriage and how she was planning to leave as soon as her kids were grown. He in turn told her about the problems plaguing his marriage, and they bonded over their shared pain. "Eventually," he said, "we started sleeping together."

The affair went on for about seven years. Then one day her husband figured out that she was fooling around. Larry said, "He called me and accused me of sleeping with his wife, but I denied it. Then he got a hold of my home number and he called my wife. He says, 'Your husband has been sleeping with my wife,' and blah-blah-blah. My wife was already very upset about many things, so she was ballistic after that."

Larry convinced her that she was being paranoid, explaining that the caller's wife was one of his clients. They were collaborating on a design project, and that's why they spent a lot of time together. "All of that was true, but it wasn't the whole story," he acknowledged. "Still, I was able to say, 'He's misinterpreting the situation because he's jealous,' blah-blah. I made up this whole story to keep her from leaving me."

Larry's wife bought his explanation, let it go, and the affair continued. "I don't know why," he said. "By that point, I was really playing with fire. I don't know if it was the thrill of getting away with it that outweighed the guilt or what, but I was crazy. I kept on. It's like you're robbing the bank, and you narrowly escape the cops, and you know they're onto you, and you keep dipping into other banks. It's not going to end well. But I was relentless. And ridiculous."

His wife got a promotion at work and became totally focused on her career and Larry and his mistress continued sleeping together. "My relationship with my wife was deteriorating more and more as we kept on going," he said. "I was kind of reaching out to somebody for comfort as the ship was sinking at home, but it doesn't help save the dying relationship to be looking for solace outside of it. But I didn't have the courage to end it. We had kids, and our lives were all tied together, and she was trying to better her life, and I was a coward."

Even after so many years, Larry did not want to leave his wife for his girlfriend. What he did want was for his relationship with his wife to change, but he didn't know how to say that. Then one day his wife found out that the relationship she had suspected was real.

"I had gotten a second phone so that none of my texts or calls would be on my regular phone," he said, "but then, one day, I left the phone in my pocket when I put my pants in the hamper. When my wife picked up the pants, the phone fell out. She was, like, 'What the fuck is *that*?' She knew I had no good reason to have two phones. She went berserk, yelling and crying. It was a mess. She called our kids into the room and told them I was cheating on her and told me I had to get out of the house, *and* I couldn't take our cars. 'You can have your whore come and pick you up!' she yelled. Then she took my second phone and called my mistress while our kids were standing right there. She didn't answer, but I was humiliated.

"*Then* my wife called one of her uncles who also lived in town, waking him up. She told him, 'He's been cheating on me for years and years,' and blah-blah-blah. He said, 'Okay, I'm coming up there, and I'm going to take care of that mofo!' That's when I got really scared, because he was a pretty violent dude."

Suddenly Larry's wife punched him. "She hit me in the face a few times, and I didn't retaliate. I asked her to let me go, but she wouldn't. Then she grabbed a pair of scissors and lunged at me, ripping my shirt. I was really afraid she was going to stab and kill me. And I was afraid her uncle was going to show up. I'm, like, 'What are my kids thinkin'?" Everything was totally out of control; this was the worst moment of my life. I grabbed her hand, knocking the scissors loose, and called 911. I told them, 'I cheated on my wife, she found out, and now she's attacking me. She's trying to stab me! I said I would go, but she won't let me leave. I think she's going to kill me. Can you come over here?' "

The police arrived and questioned both of them, but Larry was the only one who had marks on him: his shirt was slashed, his face was bruised, he was bleeding. And her palm had marks from where she'd gripped the scissors. The police arrested the wife. "That is not what I wanted," he said. "I just wanted her to stop attacking me, but once they saw what she'd done, they cuffed her."

From there, things only got worse. Larry's wife sat in jail for a day and a half. The kids were freaking out, and so was he. "I did not intend for my wife to get locked up at all. It was definitely the worst day of my life." He called a lawyer and filed for divorce. After her release, his wife filed a restraining order against him, claiming that Larry had attacked *her* and that he was a threat to the kids. The police came, took his kids away, and left them in the custody of their mother.

"That killed me," he said. "I was a devoted dad. So I started fighting to get my kids back. Her lawyer said, 'If you make this a quick divorce and agree to give up all your rights to the kids, then we'll drop the restraining order.' This is a common tactic to try to leverage a father into surrendering. But I was not about to agree to give up my kids." At the hearing for the aggravated assault charges against her, he told his lawyer that he didn't want to press charges, but it turned out to be too late for him not to. She was facing serious trouble. Again, Larry really didn't want her to go to jail, nor did he want his children to see their mother incarcerated. So, when her lawyer asked for a delay, he didn't object. But that delay and several subsequent delays meant the case was dragging on for a long while, and, all that time, Larry was barred from seeing his kids. He couldn't attend his son's eighteenth birthday party.

"It was rough. Really rough."

Eventually the divorce was finalized, but, in the process, the judge grew very disgusted with the wife. They had been ordered not to discuss the case in front of the kids and not to say negative things about each other, yet Larry's wife had ignored the judge's instructions and told the kids lots of derisive things about him. The judge responded by awarding him full custody of the kids and prohibited her from visitation unless she agreed to counseling. "I wanted her to have equal time with the kids," Larry said, "but the day the divorce was finalized, she was so mad that she stormed out of court with smoke coming from her ears. That was the last time we ever saw her."

Neither Larry nor his children have any idea where she is—he said she changed her phone number. She just disappeared. After the divorce, his life went into a real downward spiral. "I ended up filing bankruptcy, and my relationship with my children was really damaged. The damage to all of our lives has been super high. My kids didn't want anything to do with me for a while. It was very tough. One of my kids talked about suicide. And

I'm depressed because all of this mess is my fault. My wife didn't have to attack me, but she wouldn't have been that mad if I hadn't cheated. I wish I had not done any of this crap. It was definitely not worth it at all. My life came crashing down. It was horrible. It's still terrible. My kids don't have their mother, and they just have this insane memory of her in jail and this night things went nuts and all of this crap. I would tell anybody who's screwing around to stop. Just break it off before you get caught. Because getting caught can be a nightmare. The potential downside is so low it's not worth any of the fun."

I heard something similar from Matt from Detroit, who

said his affair was going along just fine until his mistress showed up at his house. "She came to my door, man. She came to where I live and knocked on my door. My wife was home. Because she was there on our doorstep, I had no idea what she was going to say. I ran and told my wife, 'I've been cheating on you.' She didn't believe me. Then she went out there and opened the door and saw this woman. Then she believed.

"After that day, I was in the doghouse at home for a while, but that was the least of my problems. This woman kept coming around, man. Over and over. I was basically being stalked. I'd be outside with my kids, and she would walk up. She followed my wife one time and then, while I was sleeping, she broke the windows on my car.

"Then she had me arrested! I had never been arrested before. I got arrested at my job. I didn't do anything, and she had me arrested. They threw me in jail, saying I had hit her. I had not hit her—I hadn't even been around her! But she said that I came to her house and hit her right before my lunch break. Total fiction. But here we go. At the time that she said I was in her house, I was at work, I had clocked in, but the cops who arrested me didn't want to hear anything about that. Next thing I know, I'm downtown behind bars with the murderers and the rapists. I got out and showed them that I had been at work during the time I supposedly attacked her, but I spent the next five years looking over my shoulder, thinking this chick was about to ruin my life again."

Justin from Phoenix didn't go to prison, nor did he come close to losing his life, but he was forced to take a lie detector test and discovered a lot more than he expected. One morning his wife woke him up and said her parents were downstairs, wanting to talk to him. The couple had been married just a short time.

"I should've known that whatever it was wasn't going to be great," Justin said, "but I went down there and acted like I was happy to see them." What he didn't know was that his wife had found out that he had been emailing back and forth with a woman he'd met on a website for hooking up. She had printed out the emails between him and this woman and given them to her parents. "I get downstairs, and they're sitting there reading some stuff and looking at me like I'm a monster, and I'm thinking, *What the fuck is going on?*"

Then he found out what they were reading: emails where he was obviously making plans to meet a woman for sex. Justin was mortified. His wife announced that she wanted a divorce. He apologized and told her that the emails weren't what she thought they were. She didn't believe him. He offered to take a lie detector test, hoping the offer would prove something (and that she wouldn't make him do it), but she said, "Great, let's do it." He said, "Okay, but you take one too." Just to make it a group thing. He had no reason to suspect her of anything, but when he said that, she started hemming and hawing, and she got really uncomfortable. Justin pressed her a bit more, and she admitted that *she* had been fooling around. That's why she was suspicious of him. Then, as their argument right in front of her parents grew more and more intense, she admitted to having slept with a second man.

"It was her dentist!" he said. "I knew the guy because she told me I should try him, and I had. We'd talked and stuff, while she's fucking him. Incredible. It was very volatile. We both had a lot of anger that we were flinging at each other."

Nevertheless, Justin wanted to try working things out. Then one night he overheard his wife talking on the phone to someone and talking in a way that made him suspicious. After she left the house, he got in his car and drove down around until he spotted her car parked on the side of the road. He waited awhile until he saw his wife and the dentist walking arm in arm toward her vehicle. Justin waited until they got in, then walked up and yanked open her door. The dentist bolted out of the passenger seat clutching a gun, came around the car, and started punching Justin. The next thing he knew, his wife had exited the driver's side to join the fray, slugging him in the face. "After that, I just said screw it and left," he said. "Our divorce was so acrimonious that my lawyer said we were the angriest couple he'd ever seen."

Jack, a former police officer from Tennessee, said he and his wife dated for five years before they got married, but he was never faithful. "I pretty much constantly cheated on her even though I really did love her and cared for her," he told me. "It was just something about appealing to another woman—a new woman—that I couldn't turn away from."

While they were still dating, he got caught cheating several times and managed to talk his way out of it. But after they tied the knot, it was a different story. When his wife found out that he had been spending time with another woman, she moved out. His wife also used the opportunity to turn the tables.

"That was the first time I ever got cheated on ever in my life," he said. "I was so upset that I went out of my mind with rage. But I was mad at myself because I knew that I had brought it all on myself. I wouldn't have been in that position if I hadn't cheated on my wife in the first place. I knew it was my fault. That's why I shot myself."

Jack had a lot of internal conflict going on then. A physician he had seen for help with chronic depression put him on antidepressant drugs that changed him in ways he didn't expect. They made him even more depressed. "I wasn't in my right mind, and I was driving by myself, and I had my gun on my seat beside me," he said. "I just grabbed it, put the gun to my chest, pulled the trigger, and it went off. I was going, like, thirty miles an hour down the street, through a light. I didn't really intend to shoot myself while I was driving, but I wasn't thinking straight." Jack turned around to see if anything got hit because he was in such shock that he still didn't realize he had shot himself.

"When I turned around, I lost my breath, and when I lost my breath, my head went down, and I saw the hole in my jacket. There was a hole in the middle of my chest. I pressed on the brakes real hard and stopped, but now everything was happening real fast—like my mind was really loud and chaotic—so I grabbed my phone, and I called my best friend. No answer. Then, I called my brother. No answer. Then I called my wife, but me and her was arguing. so she wasn't picking up the phone. I started to pass out of consciousness because the bullet had hit my lungs, then bounced around and hit the sack around my heart, and it busted a couple of inches from my spine. I kept passing out and coming to because my lung was filling up with fluid."

People ran to the car and helped get Jack to the hospital. He was whisked right into surgery. Although the doctors were able to remove the bullet, the damage was already done and he lost a lung. Jack and his wife broke up. He's got a new girlfriend now. It's pretty serious. But he's cheating on her—with his ex-wife. "She divorced me, but we never stopped talking. I know it sounds crazy—and it is—but I can't stop. It's an addiction. I can't help myself. It's a disease. Honestly, I don't really like it because it makes a monster out of people. It made me into something I hated, something I didn't want to be. That's why I shot myself. But here I am still doing the same thing."

Cheatingland is a place where you can get scarred for life.

CHAPTER EIGHT

WHY MEN LEAVE CHEATINGLAND

"I remember once driving around thinking about my wife and my girlfriend," said Nathan the actor as he recounted the moment when he realized he could no longer sleep around. "It felt like my mind was overflowing with thoughts and responsibilities, and it was onerous. I felt stressed and kind of oppressed by how much I had to remember and consider and figure out. I mean, my wife and my kids take up a lot of my mind, and then work takes up a lot of my mind, and then you add in all that goes into having a girlfriend on the side—the stuff around seeing her, the effort to keep her wanting to be with me, all the stuff that went into keeping it a secret—I felt mentally overtaxed by it all. It was taking up all of the bandwidth in my mind. I had to do all this crap to keep my two women happy. I had to make sure I checked in with them and made them feel seen, and I had to constantly brush up on my lies and rehearse them over and over. And I had to make sure my kids were good and figure out my next moves at work. Plus, my mom was sick.

"It was like my mind was a pie that was way bigger than its plate, drooping over the sides and spilling all onto the table, and you don't even know how or where to start. I felt so overstuffed with thoughts, feelings, worries, fears, lies, and all of this other stuff that I thought my brain was going to start oozing out of my ears for real. It felt like a migraine, but there wasn't any physical pain because it wasn't a real migraine; it was just, like, mind pain. I knew right there I had to give my mind a rest. I had to cut something out of my life because I couldn't handle everything that was coming at me.

"The only thing I could think of doing was eliminating my girl from my life. I didn't want to do it. I loved sneaking off with her, I really looked forward to those moments, I loved getting away with it, I loved getting it, but I didn't see any other way. I wasn't getting divorced, I wasn't abandoning my kids, I wasn't leaving my career, I couldn't put my mom on a patch of ice and push her off into the ocean. The girlfriend was the only movable part. It felt like giving up on having the crazy dessert you love, but I couldn't live with that feeling of my mind being overstuffed all the time. I had to do something. I had to, like, save me from me. So, she had to go. I didn't want to do it, but what else could I do?"

There are several reasons why men realize a life of cheating is no longer what they really want. "I had to stop because I was so stressed," said Scott from Dallas. I could hear the anxiety rush into his voice as he went back to that place. "It was really hard. My blood pressure was going up. I was having a lot of fun when I was in the same room as my other woman because I was blocking out the rest of the world and I was in the moment with her, but all those times when I wasn't with her, I was constantly super-stressed. I was always worried that my wife was about to turn to me and say, 'What the hell is this text about?' Or 'What's this picture?' Or 'Why is my friend saying her friend saw you somewhere?' Yadda, yadda, yadda. It didn't add up. The stress I was going through over all this was greater than the pleasure I was getting from it, and when I realized that, I said to myself, *What the hell are you doing?*"

For many men, there's a sense of self-disgust that triggers a dawning of conscience. Julian said, "When I look back on everything I did, it makes me sick to my stomach. It makes me sick to think about how I could have that kind of disregard for my wife. Obviously, I cared about her the whole time, even if we were having trouble. It's an awful thing to do to somebody—just an awful thing all around. And I forced my friends into awkward situations so they could cover for me. It was a mess. I can't believe I put my wife and my friends in that position. I always like to think of myself as a pretty decent person, but when I look back at that period in my life, I can't say that I was being a good person. It's insane the amount of crap I had to do to maintain this affair and not have it all blow up in my face, and I *still* had this constant fear that it would blow up in my face. I was lying daily and coming up with excuses to get out of my house for five or six hours at a time so I could spend time with my side chick, and I was just being foul.

"I was coming up with money lies and trying to figure out ways to hide my spending on her, which was hard because nowadays everything's trackable as far as money goes—every dollar has to go through a computer at some point—so there's a searchable record of everything, and if my wife starts asking, 'What did you spend a hundred dollars on here?' and 'Why was this dinner tab so big there?' I've got a problem. Sometimes I found myself sitting at work spending a ton of time brainstorming and researching ways to keep my finances hidden from my wife. I had a private account and a secret credit card, and it became a whole separate work project. What was I doing? It's crazy how much time I spent thinking through that aspect of it all. I let it take over my life. And the thing is, I knew it was crazy. When I look back on it now, it makes me sick to my stomach to think of the amount of money I went through, the time I spent, the lies I told. I was so fiendish to keep it all under wraps. When I was doing it, I thought all that crap was worth it, but now I don't think it was."

Kevin, too, felt that self-disgust. He said the exhilaration he felt when he was with his girlfriend was followed by intense shame when he was back with his wife. "When you go home to your woman after you've fucked another girl, you lay down, and you're kinda like, 'I'm disgusting.' It loses its adventurous allure and quickly devolves into disgust with yourself. You want to take a shower and wash off the woman you just had, but if you walk in the house and immediately take a shower, that will definitely raise her suspicions. You won't make her suspicious if you just sit there smelling yourself and feeling like shit, but that sucks, so, either way you're screwed."

Some cheaters told me they knew what they were doing wasn't right and felt weighed down by the stress of it all, yet they still struggled to stop. Eric from California, who's been married fifteen years and was in a single affair with someone from work, said, "Yeah, dude, I know it's wrong. I know that, and I still do it, and I wish I knew why, man." He felt the immensity of what he was doing and pulled himself out. "I had to stop," he said. "It got to my head. I started stressing out all the time. My blood pressure was going nuts because I was lying to both women. So I stopped. I had to get out of that, I had to do the right thing. It was really hard living a double life, man."

Many philanderers eventually walk away from Cheatingland even if they never get caught. Something gets to their heart. Their value system changes. The risk-versus-reward calculus stops making sense. They get tired of the chaos, no longer want the drama; they grow up and stop chasing and start focusing on their home life.

Julian said he began to feel like a jerk because of all the dishonesty. "I've always painted myself as the quintessential good person who could be trusted to be a good husband, father, coworker, all of that, and I tried to always do right by people," he said, "and one of the very few things that doesn't match that good picture of myself was the lying. Cheating requires too much lying, and every time I had to make a conscious lie, that really hurt. That really made it difficult for me to see myself as the person I wanted to see myself as."

Mark from Las Vegas told me that one day he took a step back from his life and asked himself, *Why am I screwing around? Why am I living like this?* And he didn't know. "I literally did not have an answer," he said. "It was one of those moments where you have an out-of-body experience, and you're just looking at yourself, and I didn't understand what I was looking at. I saw myself lying in this girl's bed while my wife was with the kids, and it all felt so wrong. And the worst of it was, I didn't really know why I was doing it. Like, deep down, why am I here? What am I getting out of this? Why am I taking this risk? Why am I leaving work and family to do this? If I had asked that question a moment earlier, when I was on top of her, I would've known exactly why I was there. Inside her, I felt amazing, I felt like *the man*, I felt powerful. In those moments, nothing in the world existed but her.

"But as soon as it ended, and I was lying beside her, then

the shame rushed in and the confusion rose up and the self-loathing came on—that's when I couldn't see how the thrill I'd just had was worth going through all the rest of it. I realized that the shame felt worse than the sex felt good, and the shame lasted way longer. Really recognizing that was scary. When I asked myself why I was there and why I was doing that, and I demanded a real answer from myself, I finally saw myself for the first time in a long time—like, *really* saw myself for who I really was, and I felt so fucking dirty, and I hated that feeling of not liking myself."

Harry said he had a moment of clarity arrive in the middle of sex. "I was midstroke in a chick," he said, "and it just dawned on me so hard that I wasn't living right. I said, 'I don't want to be a whore no more.' It felt like my head was inside a giant bell that had just been rung, and the reverberations of evil were just running through me, making it hard to even think. I had to get out of her. I had to stop. I pulled out and told her, 'I can't do this no more.' She's like, 'What?' She started crying. She threw on her clothes and ran out, and it was a mess, but that moment actually saved my life. It was the beginning of the best part of my life. I sat there and said, 'God, from now on, I don't want to be with women just to be with someone, and I don't want to do anything with anybody. I want to be right toward my wife.' And I just stopped. I was tired of hurting, man. I was tired of hurting others, and I was tired of being hurt."

Many men find the excitement of chasing wanes as they

grow older and the responsibilities of family mount and the fun of parenting swells. The more they acknowledge the seriousness of adulthood and the fact that lots of people they love are relying on them, the more they find that their attempt to recapture their youthful sexual glory is misplaced. The challenge of juggling all the aspects of being a grown-up is real, and quitting the cheating life is partly about growing up and leaving behind a dream world and instead accepting the value of being older and a leader for your family.

"I have a lot of shit to pay for," said a New Yorker named Charles. "I have the Westchester crib to pay for and the Hamptons place. I have cars and 401(k)s and IRAs. I've got all kinds of bills. I've got to roll my sleeves up in six dimensions. I have to open opportunities, I have to close opportunities, I've got to get the paperwork done, I've got to execute. And I've gotta come home and raise my family. I need to coach Little League for my sons. I've got to do all the things that go into being a dad, and there are only x number of hours in the day, so when do I slide that fly little missy into that mix? And what am I giving up so I can go do that? Either you're gonna not do a business deal that could land you a better situation, or you're not going to go to the game with your son, or you're not going to spend time on the couch with your wife. Which of those amazing little things do you want to give up? For me, when I took a look at my life, the answer was none of them. I didn't want to let any of that go. I couldn't. The easiest thing to give up was the poison."

While many men told me it was their fathers who slipped them the blueprint for cheating, a small number said it was their fathers who inspired them to stop. Chris said, "After I cheated, I told my dad, and he told me how stupid it was to cheat, and he said he knew it was stupid because he had cheated on my mom. We had never talked about that before, but I guess he thought it was important enough to bring out that lesson then. He told me to think about the long-term joy of having a family versus having a few minutes of pleasure. He told me to think about not being around for my son, whether it's taking him to school, or not being there to plan a birthday party, or just playing with him in the backyard. Those thoughts hit me hard. That sort of pushed me to stop doing that I was doing." But very few men were inspired to quit by their fathers. Dads often push men into this life; rarely do they pull them out.

Most men who quit changed their behavior due to one of three motivations. The third most common was a fear of losing their wives. Matt said, "One day I woke up, and the fear that I might get caught was buzzing in my ear. I was really on edge, and I thought about what would happen if my wife found out. For the first time, I thought that if she found out, she'd be destroyed. She'd be shattered. She'd be so sad. And I said, 'Holy shit, why would I want to hurt my wife? I love her. I have fun with her, she looks out for my emotional well-being, so why would I put her emotional well-being in jeopardy?' In that instance, I realized how detrimental cheating is to her, and I was, like, I'm never cheating again. And that was the end of that."

The men who told me they quit because of their wives talked a lot about karma and how they felt like they were setting themselves up for a powerful boomerang effect—maybe even a disastrous one. Jackson from LA said, "The only thing that helped me grow out of it is understanding the karmic level of it: like, Okay, you're not going to get caught for this crime, but you are going to get caught by the universe. Unless you do something to end it yourself, unless you pull the plug, then it will only end in pain. That's the only other way it can end. Somebody's getting burned. You might get burned, your wife could get burned, your girlfriend could get burned—more than likely, the lover is going to get burned over everybody, but that makes her a liability; like, is she going to retaliate and make things horrible for everyone else? You don't know. So many people are having their feelings exposed and maybe hurt, and there's going to be some karmic dues to pay at some point. You know that the bill for all your stuff is coming sooner or later."

Men in their forties and fifties are far more likely than guys in their twenties and thirties to realize there's no such thing as a free lunch. A man might pull off a secret relationship for a while—he might even escape detection forever—but he might also be hit with a very steep bill at some point. "At the end of the day," Jackson continued, "you might think you're really getting away with something, but the universe is going to make you pay. All good shit comes with a price. Nothing that great is ever free."

Stan said, "I began to think about how honorable my wife was throughout all my ridiculous behavior, and how true and good she was as a person, and how insane it was to do anything to hurt her in any way. I was putting myself in the position of hurting her every day. And even if she never found out, it wasn't fair—I'm only one person, and I've got only so much energy, and if I'm putting that energy some-place else, then I'm not putting it toward her and my family. Even if she doesn't know what I'm doing, that's still wrong. I'm shortchanging my family; I'm giving them just a piece of myself, not all of me. How can you say family is important to you and then only give them a piece of you and share the other piece with someone else outside of the family? That's so selfish.

"I'm into investing, and from an investment standpoint, if your family is your nest egg, then how are you spending part of your time building that and part of your time and part of your energy on another relationship that's going nowhere? Spending a lot of time on a relationship that's just for a mo-mentary blast is like blowing money on something stupid that depreciates immediately. It makes no sense."

The second major reason why men quit cheating is because they're scared of their children finding out what they've done and looking down on them. The fear of being humiliated in front of the kids loomed large in the minds of many men, a lot of whom said they couldn't bear to imagine the disgrace and shame of having their children hear the story of them cheating and looking at them in disgust. They couldn't handle the thought of their children being angry at them. They want their children to look up to them. They know children see their parents as a guide for their lives— kids hear what parents say, but they put even more weight on what parents do. No one wants to be their kids' cautionary tale. Rapper Jay-Z famously cheated on his superstar wife Be-yonc√© and then made a song "4:44" apologizing about it in which he said, "And if my children knew / I don't even know what I would do / If they ain't look at me the same / I would probably die with all the shame."

Many cheaters said they were far more motivated to stop because they worried about the effect on their children more than on their wives. "I feared hurting my kids," said Josh, a married man who's had several affairs. Like many husbands, Josh hated the thought of his actions changing his kids' lives. "I feared that if my wife found out, we would end up in a divorce and split the family apart, and I didn't want that for my kids. So I stopped."

Jackson: "The birth of my daughters really opened up something for me. I realized that my actions were going to be felt by them. I saw that there was going to be karmic dues to pay and that, with kids, there was going to be a brand of my family. And me, as the leader of that brand, needed to be held to certain standards. Plus, I wanted them to live their lives in truth, and how can I preach that when I'm not living my life in truth? When you live your life in truth, you get certain rewards out of it. You get to feel good about yourself, and the pride you feel about yourself helps you operate with courage throughout the rest of your life. You can't have real pride in yourself if you're a liar. If you're a liar, there's no way you can feel one hundred percent good about yourself because you haven't integrated your whole self into one thing.

"My daughters got me thinking about all of that and made me say, 'Nah, I have to do something different. I can't risk hurting their lives because I need more fun and excitement.' They say having kids makes some men grow up, and it definitely made me take a look at my life and realize I needed to be better. I mean, I would never purposely hurt their bodies—like, I'd never drop them, I'd never put them in the car without a seatbelt. Okay, so then how could I put their minds and their spirits at risk with my fooling around?"

For men who think they're running the risk of losing their kids, the pain of that idea was too deep to continue on with any affair, no matter how electric the sex. Chris from Chicago who had numerous girlfriends before deciding to stop fooling around, said, "I think it was just the good side of me finally saying, 'Hey! Cut the shit and take care of your family, like you're supposed to!' My oldest son was seven, and I had a five-month-old, and I just said to myself that the last thing I want is to be the daddy that's coming over to see his kids or the daddy you see just on holidays.

"I still slipped up a little after that, and I felt like an addict trying to get out of the grip of this thing, but then I said, 'I can't be jeopardizing everything I worked for over the last ten years. I can't let my bad impulses wreck my kids' lives.' You know? Because if it got out, and I had to go live somewhere else, my kids would tell that story forever: 'When I was such-and-such an age, my parents got divorced because my dad was cheating.' That would become a benchmark in their lives, like a place where the story of their lives turned in a different direction. I couldn't have that happen, not over some chick. After I started to see it like that, I got it all behind me."

For men who experienced divorce in their childhood homes, the vision of getting divorced on account of their actions can inspire a ton of guilt because they know how hard all of that can be on kids. But they also worry about missing out on the little things: all the smiles and laughs and baths and breakfasts and milestones and hugs that make parenting so deeply rewarding, and not being with them every day can be painful.

Peter, who got divorced after his affair was uncovered, said, "I was extremely crushed at the idea of not being with my kid when he woke up in the morning. I grew up in a stable family, and I always thought that family was the most important thing, so to go through the disintegration of my family and knowing it was my fault because I couldn't stop screwing around, that was crushing. I was bereft for a long time, and I couldn't stop thinking about the ways I had changed his life by not being there all the time. It was really hard."

The number one reason why men decided to quit the cheating life—the reason more men gave than any other—was so that they could focus on their career. A lot of men are socialized to see job performance as one of the ways that masculinity is measured. Their career forms the core of their identity. It shapes who they are in the world and how they're able to provide for their family. That doesn't mean the man who makes the most money wins, though surely that ethos is part of it. But, at least in America, so much of how you're seen by society, not to mention how you see yourself, is wrapped up in your work—you are what you do.

Scott from Dallas said, "If you ask some of the most successful people what they do in their free time, I guarantee you it's not chasing women. I'm sure women are coming at them, but they're focused on working. I tell my boys all the time, 'Hey, man, put down the hos for one season and watch what happens. You'll have more time, more focus, more money, and less headaches. You don't have to think about *What is this woman thinking? How do I keep her happy?* You don't have to think about *What do I have to do for her birthday?* and *How can I keep it secret from my wife?*'

"The holidays took over my mind thinking about what was I gonna do to make her happy on, say, Christmas, when I couldn't be there. I spent so much time thinking about *When am I going to have to take you out on a date, and how can we get back to bed?* Now I don't have to think about those things, and I can focus on my paper. I don't spend time staying up all night, trying to get some and being half asleep the next day while other people are getting money. I don't waste my time anymore, and that helps me to be truly successful in what I do." When Seth was younger, he wanted to keep up with his friends and have as many women as them, but getting older pushed him to change his values. "Me and my guys can still hang together," he said, "but I don't have to follow what they're doing. If they're getting ass, let 'em have it. I'm getting money."

Dominic from San Jose decided he had to cut his infidelities out of his life when he opened a new business. He said, "I'm an old man who's focused on other stuff. To be honest, once I stopped doing all that chasing and dating and sleeping around, I was able to focus on school and then start doing my own little business. I was able to get more focused on me. My mind was spending a lot of time working on how to get more women and how to keep the women I have happy, and to be honest, this dude told me, 'Man, if you stop focusing on your dick, you could do something out here.'

"So that's what I did. He was right."

Brett from Seattle said, "I don't do it much anymore mainly because I'm pretty busy with my work. I'm self-employed, and I just don't have a lot of time to fit that other stuff in. It's just not more important than securing my future." Connor said, "I started working for myself about seven years ago, and

I have to do everything for my business. It's not a nine-to-five thing. I work from the time I open my eyes until the time I doze off. I don't have time to figure out how to get other women."

Roman, a married man who slept with six women before he quit straying, said, "I stopped when my work took on more importance in my mind than my dick. For most of my adult life, my penis was having a better life than I was. And once I started unpacking that, I stopped looking to women to fulfill me and started looking to my work to fulfill me. I wanted to grow up and be a man. I used to think being a man meant having lots of women, but then I realized that was boyish—that was lots of playtime. When I realized that being a grown man was about being great in my career and taking care of my work and my bills and providing for my family, then that became way more interesting than the cute chick at the end of the bar."

For men, choosing to focus on business over one's sex life is about maturing as a man. Providing for family is a central way for a man to demonstrate his love and fulfill his responsibility to his little tribe. Guys who push themselves away from the smorgasbord of sex and recommit themselves to their work are pledging to be the best man and the most fruitful provider they can be. They're choosing to not divide their time between work that benefits their family and risky playtime. They're also making a commitment to bringing peace into their lives. The chaos of the cheating life may be fun for younger men—and for those who cling stubbornly to their youthful impulses—but men who are more mature see great value in not living with the constant fear of being caught. They put value in not risking what's important. More mature men value stability and peace. They see their family as their wealth, and they won't gamble with that.

The core reason why many men quit cheating is that they stop missing their playboy days and stop longing for their younger selves and the freedom of their sex-filled, carefree twenties. They move on from cheating when they start valuing the precious moments of their family life so much that even the thrills of Cheatingland pale in comparison. When they decide that the pleasures of fatherhood and family are way more important than the joys of wild sex—not equal to it, but a clear cut above it—then they walk away from fooling around on their own.

But a big part of the rationale behind why men make the decision to be unselfish is, well, selfish. They want to focus on their career, bring in as much money as they can, and bask in the glory of being the successful breadwinner. The self-centeredness of men, and the pursuit of applause and affirmation, shape both the choice to cheat (*I want to feel like The Man by having a virtual harem*) and the choice not to cheat (*I want to feel like The Man by succeeding at work and bringing home the money my family needs*). Love for him is conditional, based on either how many women he can lure into bed or how much money he can make. Part of why he leaves home is to feel better about himself by acquiring more women, and part of why he returns is to feel better about himself by pulling in more money. In both scenarios, the man feels valued for what he does and what he creates rather than who he is inherently.

The sense of calm that descends on people who leave Cheatingland is profound. As Seth told me, "Once I stopped doing it, I realized how easy life can be when you have just one chick."

No one, however, realized that as much as Robert, the media executive. He and his wife had

"a failed marriage," he said, "but I didn't have the balls to pull the trigger and file for divorce because, frankly, it was easier to just do my thing and not disrupt my home. So, I was chasing women. It was easy because I was on the road a lot for work. It became like a game." He was a typical Peacock, seeing women as a challenge and each interaction as a contest.

"I wouldn't call women when I was making travel plans, or even the day before I arrived. No, I would wait until the plane landed on the tarmac and then start texting women in that town and see who responded first. These were pre-established relationships where they knew the deal: we're not going to the movies. Meet me in my hotel room. Usually, in my work, I land late and leave early, and they knew that. Emotionally, I was so disconnected that it was easy. I was addicted to having moments of intimacy with people I had not created relationships with. There's a biological rush to new connections, and I was living for that high. I felt schizophrenic because I was only looking to fuck, but I didn't want women to feel like I had only fucked them, so there was a weird combination of being just warm enough to fake like there was a connection but still being cold and distant enough that real intimacy didn't develop. I was fucked up." He was playing with fire. Then he got caught.

"Everything got real when I got this girl pregnant," Robert continued. "It happened the last time we had sex. I decided I was done with her, and I cut it off, and then she called me back and said she was pregnant. I did the typical 'How do you know it's mine?' But deep down, I knew it was mine. I begged her not to have it because I was married with kids. This child I would hardly ever see. I couldn't be a deadbeat dad. That sounded horrible to me.

"While that drama was playing out, I met someone else and legitimately fell in love with her. Talk about a quagmire. I couldn't leave my wife for this new woman I loved. I couldn't have my kids have a stepmother who'd broken up my marriage. I don't care what kind of fantasyland you live in, you're not having a blended family that includes the woman who ended your first marriage. The drama went on and on for months until my pregnant friend had the baby. It looked more like me than my older kids did! My mother saw a picture of the kid and said, 'That's definitely your son.' It was absurd."

It got worse. And, like a Peacock, Robert seemed to al-most revel in the drama, the chaos, and the many women focusing on him. "My wife had a sense that I was fooling around, so one day when I was out, she went through my boxes, and, of course, she found stuff. I was in a hotel when I got a text from my new girlfriend: 'Why is your wife calling my phone?'

"I had no idea.

I called home. She said, 'Who is this woman? You told her you're in love with her? What the fuck is going on?'

"I tap-danced out of that and called my girlfriend, who said she wanted to call back my wife.

I was so relieved to finally be caught, I said okay.

"My girlfriend said, 'I'm not going to lie to her.'

"I said, 'I don't want you to. I've had enough.'" Robert had loved the craziness enough to let things get way out of con-trol, but now that he'd been caught, he was ready to release the craziness. "I was tired of constructing and remembering lies and running the whole three-ring circus that I'd cre-ated," he said. "I hung up and sat there knowing that my wife and my girlfriend were talking, but I was so over the stress and anxiety that I was happy that it was out in the open, and I was done. That was the end of all three relationships. I started fresh and left all the madness behind. I see my son sometimes, but I have no relationship with his mom."

Robert took all of that very hard and had a tough time reawakening himself. "When everything hit the fan, and both my wife and my girlfriend were, like, 'Fuck you,' and my baby was being born, with all of that happening at once, I went through a major bout of depression. It was such a deep, intense cloud of darkness that I didn't realize it was depression until after I came out of it. There was a good four to six months of feeling like I didn't want to leave the house, I had no interest in seeing anybody, and I really thought about ending my life. The whole thing.

"But when I started to date again, I was not feeling stress, I was not feeling the pressure of the game, and it was a really welcome change, and that clarity of mind let me be open to meeting my current wife. By the time I met her, I was never tempted to sleep around because I'd had enough of relationships where I was running around and juggling women and all that. This time I had no stress, and I loved it. I enjoyed being with one person. My relationship was so much healthier and more fulfilling because I was able to really give myself fully to her. Because I wasn't on the hunt.

"I enjoyed not having to hide my phone. I enjoyed knowing who I was gonna see every day. I enjoyed the focus and the productivity that came from using my downtime not as hunting season but to read, or write, or rest, which made me feel like a happier person. My relationship was honest, it was open, we were real friends, and I wasn't doing her dirty and feeling bad about it and having all these up-and-down feelings about myself. My mind was at peace because I was never afraid of getting caught. I didn't have voices in the back of my mind saying, 'You're doing something wrong.' To not feel that stress, to not feel the pressure of the game was a welcome change.

"But it's also about having the right relationship," he said. "When you do, it's like an endless source of meat. When you're bagging the wrong chicks, you're just getting Cornish hens. You get two bites, and then you need something else. But I found a relationship where so much of what I needed and wanted was in the same person. But I'm telling you, it was one of those things where we were dating, and I had to consciously say to myself, *I gotta cut these relationships off. I can't have these extra things.* Because it's easy to do that, and for me, as soon as something goes a little bad, I'm making a call. But I stopped doing that, before we got married. I started giving the relationship a chance to have ups and downs and stick with it through the downs. I think it makes a big difference when you're staying focused through the downs rather than spreading your energy somewhere else."

Robert was so serious about staying on the right path that when he remarried, he consciously constructed a life infrastructure that would help keep him on the straight and narrow. Like a recovering addict, he built a support system. "You look at the five people that you spend the most time with, and you see a reflection of yourself," he said. "So, I had to modify who's part of my inner circle and let it be a reflection of creating this consistency with what I say I want. That's how I've been in a place where I don't fall for the shit that I used to do.

"That doesn't mean I'm not tempted," he said. "It doesn't mean I don't see attractive women, it doesn't mean that women don't come up to me, it doesn't mean there aren't times when I'm, like, 'Maybe I should hit that.' It was a slow process, man. It wasn't just one day I was, like, 'Yo, I don't want to cheat no more. It was a process, it was a grooming process, it was a training process, and now it's a management process.

"I remember one night I was hanging out at a club with a celebrity, a man who has legions of residual chicks. I end up dancing with this girl. You know when you have energy with somebody, and I wasn't married yet, but I was close enough to being engaged that I knew it was inappropriate. So we danced, I had a good number of drinks, and we exchanged numbers. But when I woke up, I said nah, and I never called her. Then, maybe two weeks later, she texts me and said, 'Hey, I thought I would've heard from you by now.' And I almost had a heart attack. I was like, 'Oh my God, what did I do, I can't believe the chick just texted me this, I gotta erase this number, and I realized that I had so separated myself from the game—I didn't even have a heart for it no more—that I felt bad about her texting me. Which is what I prefer.

"I wanted this new peace to become a constant in my life, so I created an ecosystem of monogamy where all my friends are friends with my wife, I go almost everywhere with my wife, and if she doesn't come, I've got men in my life who accept that I don't want to be out there screwing around anymore, and they hold me accountable. I used to have friends who *helped* me cheat. I don't hang out with those guys anymore. My friends now help me avoid temptation. It's not like cock blocking, it's more like, if I start to think about making a move, they're there to remind me how much nicer life is without all those complications, without all that stress. They'll jump in when I'm talking to a girl and make sure it all stays on the right path. They'll give me that look that says, 'You don't need it.' The vibe in my crew isn't that a real man has women, the vibe is that a real man has *one* woman, and loyalty is cool. It's easier to stay on the right path when you've got accountability mechanisms all around you, and when you have friends who aren't into that and won't allow you to get away with it. If I have a moment of weakness, they'll keep me right. In my old group, I told them, 'I'ma be a hunter,' and they helped me be a hunter. Now I'm telling them, 'I want to be faithful, and if you see me slipping, I want you to help.' They do, and now I never worry about someone popping up and ruining my world."

Harry, a Dead Bedroomer, used to run around with multiple girlfriends in addition to his wife. Now, he said, "I wake up with a clear conscience, I go to bed with a clear conscience. I'm not worried about, you know, somebody calling or texting or whatever while I'm out with my family and saying, 'Hey, I need to see you' or 'When we gonna hook up again?' That kind of stuff is exciting up to a certain point, but then it's, like, *damn*. You gotta keep trying to think of an excuse to leave the house, you gotta cover that up, and it gets to be too much work."

Several men who were caught said they ended up feeling tremendous relief putting behind them the stress of worrying about being found out. Zac, a reformed Peacock from Pennsylvania, said, "After a while of screwing around, you become mentally drained, and then you become physically drained. Especially if you happen to live in a small town, you're always wondering if you're going to run into that person while you're out with your family. You wonder if maybe they'll turn psycho and show up at your doorstep and break into your house or some kind of shit like that. Nowadays, anything can happen."

Nowadays, Zac teaches his sons to be faithful. "I tell them, 'Don't be a man whore. It's not necessary. It doesn't make you a man to go out and have multiple girlfriends, multiple sex partners, or that type of thing.'"

After they got off the roller coaster, many men reflected back and decided it wasn't worth it. Harry said, "One thing I wish I could go back and change is the stuff I did. I would take it all back. I wouldn't cheat one single time because, at the end of the day, it wasn't worth it. One, it was physically taxing; two, it was expensive as shit; three, it was very damaging to her. I wish I could go back and tell myself, 'Dude this isn't going to end well!' And it's not like I don't get the urges now. I mean, man, there's women everywhere! I see pretty women every day. But I can't hurt my wife again. I can't go back to that." The relief of not having to chase or plot or worry is powerful. "At the time, it felt empowering," Bill said. "But now that I look back on it, I'm, like, *What were you doing?* I went back read some of the emails I sent, and it made me feel sick to my stomach. So, hopefully guys can recognize and appreciate both the good stuff that's going to happen with this and the emotional downsides that can happen. Now I have a lot of feelings of regret and shame."

Shame may arise in cheaters who realize that a man's infidelity is corrosive for their wives but also counterproductive for themselves. Robert said, "I don't think that as men we're really cognizant about what indiscriminate cheating does to us. I think that there's this inherent debate around whether monogamy is natural, and that's really just a convenient way of saying fucking around is just what men do. But I think that there are some of us who have a desire to create a level of intimacy that we've never felt, and when we're cheating, we never open ourselves up to legitimate intimacy because you're never truly vulnerable."

Also, he said, what's the endgame? When does the hunting end? "The question isn't why we need to hunt, it's when do we realize we've got it? Most of us who need to hunt never say all we want is one kill. We've said to ourselves, 'I want more, I'm gonna kill as much as I can.' That's what the fuck hunters do. Most of us are not Ahab out on the sea looking for one great whale, like, 'Oh my God, if I get this whale, I'm done forever.' We'll take whales, we'll take minnows, we'll take plankton—whatever the fuck comes up on the boat is fine. So how do you know when to stop hunting?"

For men who quit, it's not a phase, it's an evolution. Men who told me they decided to stop stepping out on their wives did not fall back into the cheating life. Isaac, who had a two-year affair while he was married, said, "I started to ask myself if it was worth. I'd go through all this trickery and lying to get to a moment of sex, and, as soon as it was over, I'm breathlessly grabbing my phone, hoping my wife hadn't called me during the act to tell me something happened, and because I hadn't picked up, she'd be, like, 'Why didn't you pick up? Where were you?' And then I'd have to come up with another lie. So I'd automatically start thinking of a lie whenever I scooped up my phone, and my head was full of my lies, which felt crazy.

"When I was at home, I was always afraid that I'd get a text from the girl when the wife was right beside me, or she'd see it before I did, so I was always looking over my shoulder and nervous all the time. Is the sex worth all that? Probably not. I know guys that have whole different phones and a whole other phone plan and a bill that goes somewhere other than their home attached to a phone that they don't even bring out until certain times when they need to fool the wife. That's like Mafia-level cat and mouse trickery. Is it really worth it if you need to do all of that to get away with it? If you feel like you've got to act like you're in the CIA just to get some extra pussy, you may need to rethink your life.

"I used to think it was part of the price to get some strange but now, I don't think it's worth it. I pride myself on being up front about my life and my choices in every aspect of my life except for this one, and I started to see myself as a hypocrite because I was sneaking around doing all this shit over here, while preaching to myself that I was an honest person. I had to leave all that behind."

Men who decided to quit on their own sounded lighter and more at ease because they were liberated from dealing with the wild ups and heavy downs of cheating—the excitement, the fear, the dopamine, the shame. They have nothing to worry about anymore, and the calm that produces was apparent in their voices on the phone. "I wake up with a clear conscience," said Michael from Denver who had many affairs before he quit the life. "I go to bed with a clear conscience. I'm not worried about somebody calling or texting or whatever while I'm out with my family and saying, 'Hey, when we gonna hook up again?' and having to think of some excuse to leave the house and then figuring out how to cover it all up. I have a lot more space in my mind to think about things that aren't so devious. I feel my body being more relaxed than it has been in years; I didn't even know I was tense before, but I was because I was constantly on pins and needles thinking of how to close up any loose ends and wondering when I was going to be found out. Now I can relax because I have nothing to hide. When my wife asks to use my phone, I can hand it to her without fear. That feels really nice."

But some men continue to feel temptation. Despite making the mature, family-focused decision and sticking to it, some men still found it hard to not fall back. They know what makes the most sense for them and their family, and they live by that, yet they can hear the street—or the sheets—calling. Charles, who was a model of maturity when he said he would rather attend his son's baseball game and kiss his daughters good night and sit on the couch with his wife instead of having crazy sex with another woman, said he has never gone back on that choice. But, he acknowledged openly, sometimes he struggles with it.

"It's like I'm an addict getting over some shit," Charles said. "I mean, I see the opportunities and the pathways to get some all the time. I'm like a chess player who can see four or five moves ahead. I know how the game goes, and I see it happening right in front of me. Like, I'm out of town, I see a girl, I see the opportunity, and then I play it out in my mind. I say something clever. She says something coy. We go to dinner the next night. I tell some jokes. I tell some engaging stories. She laughs. She leans in. I start popping game. She invites me back. We do the thing. The next day, I confess all my truths to her. Down the road, her feelings get hurt. She's salty, but maybe we remain friends, maybe not.

"I know how the story goes. I can make it happen like LeBron in the open court on a fast break— but I don't follow that playbook anymore because I make an active decision to not go down that road. I want the family stuff; I don't want to mess that up for anything. That's not who I was a few years ago, but it's who I am now. I mean, when I think back on what I did, all the hotel rooms I saw, for all of that, what did I get? What did I really get? I got nothing. And what did I give up? A lot. What did I risk? Everything. If my kids were living in another house and I didn't wake up and see them every morning because I needed some extra, I'd be devastated.

"But still, I think about what could be, and how much fun it would be for a night to be with some girl instead of being alone or whatever, and I have to struggle and be really mindful to say no to certain situations and conversations in order to keep myself from going down that road. It's easy as hell to slip down that road. Like, an alcoholic has a voice inside telling him, 'Hey, you can have just one drink! Okay, now have just one more!' Well, I have a voice inside me saying, *Hey, you're just saying hi to her, you're just having dinner with her, you're just going back to her room to have a drink, you're just gonna sleep with her once, it's okay, it's not that bad, it's just once, it's just twice.* I have to put in some work to make that voice shut up."

CHAPTER NINE

WHAT HAPPENS WHEN CHEATERS GET CAUGHT?

If having an affair is like putting a nuclear bomb in the living room, then the revelation of the affair is that bomb exploding and turning everyone and everything in that living room into dust. Under the shadow of a mushroom cloud, everyone in the family would need to stop and acknowledge that their world had changed forever. They might be able to put it back together, they might not.

Either path is possible if the couple accept that everything is different now, and they're essentially in a new phase of their marriage. If they can honestly assess what happened and talk through what they need, then they could have a future together. But if they can't be open and honest, then it's probably going to crumble at some point, if not right away. Many couples survive the revelation of an affair. How do you do it? Let me tell you the story of two married couples where the husband was cheating. These two couples—Fred and Rosa, and Ryan and Vanessa—had two different ways of coping after the affair was revealed, resulting in two very different results.

Fred is a salesman in Florida who had never had much luck with women before he met Rosa, who grew up in Hawaii. They married and had two girls. They made it through ten years of marriage, but, after two kids, they had fallen into a bit of dead bedroom rut and seemed to be drifting apart. Then came one fateful summer when Rosa and the girls flew to Hawaii to visit her sick mother while Fred stayed home. Rosa's mother took a turn for the worse and she ended up staying in Hawaii for months.

Back at home, Fred was restless. He used his time alone to go out to bars, met someone, and quickly began sleeping with her. The affair turned torrid. They began seeing each other as much as possible. But Fred was sloppy. He brought her home at night, and several neighbors saw him stumble out of a cab with a woman in a short dress on his arm and go into his house.

Word got back to Rosa that something might be going on. She called Fred. He denied everything. She heard more rumors. He still denied everything. Finally, after her mother passed, Rosa and the kids flew home. When she got there, she could tell that Fred's mind was elsewhere. She confronted him again. He told her that she was crazy. He said maybe the painkillers she was on were clouding her mind and making her suspicious and giving her anxiety. She believed him, but he was going out at night a lot, far more than before she went away, and he was staying out late. When she asked, he said it was business, but she didn't think that was true.

Rosa kept asking, and eventually Fred admitted to the affair. What's more, he told his wife that he loved the other woman and wasn't going to stop seeing her. He liked the way she made him feel. She made him feel like more of a man. Shortly after, Fred and Rosa separated and then divorced.

Fred responded to being caught without humility, grace, or honor. He was unrepentant as he thumbed his nose at his partner and all but announced that he was unwilling to do any of the work necessary to put things back together because he had moved on to a new relationship. The shit had hit the fan, and he wasn't going to help clean up. He wasn't going to talk about what had happened or how he felt. He wasn't curious enough about Rosa's feelings even to listen to her. He shut down, acted all indignant, and refused to give the relationship a chance to survive. Tragically, Fred is a normal American male. In a crucial moment, he refused to talk about his feelings, and his marriage promptly fell apart. It doesn't have to be this way.

Ryan, Vanessa's husband, reacted to getting caught in a totally different manner. A nightclub promoter in San Francisco, he met and married Vanessa when they were young. As his career grew, he used it as a way to chase women. Ryan is a Peacock who had lots of brief affairs until the day that Vanessa found out. In a tear-filled scene, she demanded he tell her all the gory details.

Ryan recalled, "She was, like, 'Tell me everything. I want to know. It hurts me, but I want to know.' He sat there and laid it all out, story after story of all his affairs and flings and one-night stands.

His words pierced Vanessa's heart like daggers, each one wounding her a little more, but Ryan knew he had to do it to stay married. As he said to me, "You can't be like the song 'It Wasn't Me,' [by Shaggy]. You gotta admit it because not having that clarity puts the other person in a weird place. It creates a lot of chaos not knowing. It creates a lot of chaos with her knowing everything, too, don't get me wrong, but . . ."

Vanessa thought she would die as he told her about all the women, but she did not. Their relationship did not die either. It was like they were burning their marriage to the ground so that they could start anew. "Once I admitted to it, we started rebuilding," Ryan said. "I promised to not make a mistake like that again, and we kind of started over, and we accepted to go forward." Ryan's openness and his honesty allowed his wife to know and understand what he had done and why. It let her see that it wasn't her fault. And now no stranger would be able to tell her something she didn't know already about her husband. It let her see her man in a fresh light as someone who, in a critical moment, would do the right thing and be honest. Yes, Ryan had screwed up by cheating on her, but this was a moment of intense pressure where their lives were at a fork. It was crunch time for their relationship, and he stepped up and showed her enough respect, love, and honor to be honest about what he had done.

He was also humble. Looking back, Ryan said, "We had a kid, and there was a natural commitment on my part to doing whatever I had to do to keep the marriage. I chose to marry her, and I still loved her, so I had to put my tail under my butt and take everything that came. I had to take it. It'd be too macho to say, 'I did what I did, take it or leave it.' I couldn't just do that to her. I made a mistake. I made a lot of mistakes, and I had to deal. She wanted to confront it, and she was in a better place when she found out everything for real. I think the position I took was helpful in terms of taking the blame and being honest. You gotta accept that you fucked up and take the hits. That kept the marriage going."

They made it through, and they're still married. Years have passed since all of that happened, and now they're happy together. Most of the time, at least. Vanessa's pain regarding Ryan's cheating did not just disappear. "To this day, I gotta deal with it," he said. "It never goes away. If it comes up, I hope that she breezes through it quickly. I try to avoid the convo. If she gets into it, I just stay quiet. There's nothing I can say to defend myself. You're never able to totally fix it. It's an emotional scar that's always on the surface. She's always reminded of it eventually. If she gets into certain feelings, she brings it up, and she slams me down. But it's been pretty good since then." Being honest was hard, but that alone saved his marriage.

Most cheaters, though, say that if they get caught, they'll deny it no matter what. Their motto: 'Never confess.' The ethos of "Deny till you die" is a rock-solid part of the cheater's code. Paul said, "You never admit it. No matter what happens, you cannot tell the truth. No matter how close they get. I could've won the Academy Award with my performances. I made up so many lies and stories it was ridiculous. It didn't make me feel good, but I had to follow that rule because if you admit it, you've got a whole other problem." Cheaters love to tell tales about how their wife looked them square in the eye, and they denied it.

Exhibit A, Mark. "I think my wife knows that I cheated on her," he said, "but I'll never admit it to her. I may mention something about another woman or look at another woman, and she'll say, 'Well, you cheated on me, so what difference does it make?' But no matter what she says, I will deny the fact that I cheated." Why? "Because it keeps her around."

One man I interviewed referenced a 2001 movie written, directed, and produced by John Singleton. "There was a line in *Baby Boy* where the wife said, 'You lied to me,' and he said, 'I lied to you because I love you. I tell my other hoes the truth 'cause they don't matter.'" Cheaters don't tell their wives the truth because they're afraid of losing them. They believe that if they come clean, all hell will break loose, the relationship will end, and their lives will change.

Christian from Miami verbalized the fear harbored by every man in the study: "I'd rather not get caught. I'd rather not hurt anybody. I'd rather not damage my own reputation. I mean, if I were caught, it might get ugly. She might be upset, but I can deal with that, but to have to deal with a nasty divorce, alimony, and her walking away with half of my stuff? That is terrifying. I don't want to be like Tiger Woods and have your whole life go from the shadows to front street and have everyone all in your business and give up your life and everything and be embarrassed in front of everyone."

Sam from New Orleans got caught after years of cheating while on real trips and fake trips. He, too, was not honest, and it cost him everything. "Oh, the miracles of Facebook," he said. "My girlfriend wrote to my wife and said, 'Hi, I'm Sam's girlfriend.' She finally thought, *I've just gotta call a spade a spade.* My wife immediately called her and said, 'That's very interesting,' and they compared notes. 'Where were you on this date or that date?' 'Oh, I was in Mexico with Sam.' 'That's interesting; he told me he was on a golfing trip with his friend.' They went through month after month after month after month.

" 'What did he get you for Christmas?'

" 'What did he get you for Valentine's Day?'

"All of this crap. It was horrible. I had been trying to prevent anything like this from happening," Sam said. "I had both of their Facebook passwords, so that if either of them reached out to the other, I could jump in and delete the message. I also had both of their email passwords, so I knew exactly how to stop anything. And I checked their pages multiple times a day just to make sure one hadn't reached out to the other.

"But that day, I was out of town at a work function, and I went to an office happy hour. For one hour. And in that sixty minutes, they wrote each other, connected, and started their phone conversation and a whole friendship. It was like the FBI and the IRS going through my records and building a case against me while I was unaware that I'd wandered into the crappy part of the movie where it's just a matter of time before I get caught. Really, you could say I was caught but just didn't know it yet.

"I came out of the happy hour, and I started calling each of them just to say hi. No response. Waited awhile, called again. Phone's going to voice mail. Texted both of them, got crickets. After awhile it was, like, *This is a long time for both of them not to respond. This is weird. This feels all wrong.* I checked online, and I didn't see anything because they had already erased their tracks, but I knew something was wrong. They'd literally talked for four hours while I was wandering around like an idiot wondering when one of them would respond to me.

"When I finally got the phone call from my wife, it was really lame. She was so mad. She was yelling, 'You're busted!

You're busted!' I didn't get it; it didn't sound real to me until she started saying, 'I know where you were! I know where you were!' That's when I realized, *Oh my God, they've just talked*. She hung up on me, and then my girlfriend called me bawling. She knew I had a wife, but once she found her conscience, it was all too stressful for her. She dumped me. Then my wife called me crying and said we're through.

I knew I should go home, but I didn't really want to, and I had to be on this trip for two more days. I was too critical to the company, and there were too many clients for me to leave. But my home life was blowing up like Vietnam. And the next day, these two are trying to be friends and make sure that I know it. Like, they met up and took a bunch of pictures where they were smiling and hugging each other, and they posted them all over Facebook. Suddenly all of my friends are calling, like, 'Yo, what is going on?' It's like a total meltdown in my social bubble because my worlds collided, so that all happened; it was a mess.

"But by the time I got back home, my wife was, like, 'What's really going on? Tell me.' I looked at her, and you know what I did? Lie, lie, lie. Hide, hide, hide. Deny, deny, deny. I admitted to a few things, but I'm a lawyer, so I just went to court and knocked down every piece of evidence that my girlfriend had thrown into the court and testified on my own behalf like never before. I knew what the jury wanted to hear, and I just laid it on thick. And somehow, after the performance of my life, we stayed together.

"But it was a mess because she didn't totally believe me, and she always had questions and suspicions, and she was always watching and doubting me. Now when I went on real work trips, I felt crappy, and I felt ashamed, and I felt her doubting me, and I was looking over my shoulder, like, *Is she watching? Is she calling? How is she keeping tabs on me today?* I was so stressed that I couldn't even think about fooling around, and I couldn't be happy even when I was at home. I couldn't be myself. It was terrible. Almost two years after that, we finally broke up. We never recovered. It's like the moment of finding out never really ended, it just carried on slowly for years after, as if I were trapped in that moment."

Sam wasn't honest, he never came clean, so he and his wife kept thinking about his affairs. They remained stuck in that moment. If cheaters and wives don't purge themselves of the details, the images, and the feelings, they can stay frozen in that moment of trauma for a long time and have to deal with a sort of post-traumatic stress disorder.

Seth got caught too. But, like Ryan, "I stopped everything, and I came clean and fessed up to my wife," he said. "I had to get it out. I told her everything like I was vomiting out this horrible meal I'd gorged on behind her back. I knew it would hurt her, and I didn't know if she'd ever talk to me again, but I had to get it out and start getting beyond it and stop being in fear of it. I had to do the right thing because living foul was eating me up inside."

Harry too got caught and decided that his wife deserved

the truth. "Try and talk from the heart about your real objective truth about yourself—like, really examine what you really wanted outside your marriage," he said. "Otherwise I think you're just being a coward. Tell her, 'This is what I was doing, this is who I was with, and this is why,' and let the chips fall where they may. Own your desires. Own what you did. Own what you want to do." It's not enough for a man to say, 'Here's who I was with and where.' He's got to dig into himself and explore *why* he did it. If he's bold enough to cheat, he should be bold enough to tell his wife the real reasons why. If he hasn't yet figured out if he's a Dead Bedroomer or a Peacock or a Completer or whatever, he should take some time to reflect on that and let her know. Each type of cheater must take stock of his motivation for cheating, and when he understands himself and why he broke their martial vows, he and his wife can begin talking and taking steps toward putting the marriage back together—or separating—with a full understanding of what happened.

It's not fair to walk away, leaving a wife thinking it was her fault and what if she had only . . . when, in reality, it was really about the influence of his dad. Or his getting rejected by women when he was younger. Or any number of other deep-seated reasons. Explaining why he cheated will help both members of the couple move forward. Michael from Denver, said, "I had to sit my wife down and spill the beans on the situation as best I could without hurting her too badly. I apologized and said that from here on out, I'm going to be the best father and best husband I can be. And we decided to move on and leave what I did in the past."

A cheater can tell his wife everything and stay married—if he's painfully honest and shares until it hurts. Then they have a better chance of pulling through and building a relationship that's much stronger. If the cheater is willing to look deeply into himself and do the hard work to really understand himself, he does not know what he'll find. Several men told me their self-exploration led them to realize that they slept with other women in part because of some residual pain from being rejected by their mother long ago.

As Eddie from Pittsburgh put it, "I think a lot of guys cheat because they're looking for something to replace what happened with their mom or something like that. They're looking for intimacy in the form of motherly type love. You know the feeling you get when you're cuddling after? It's very intimate. In some ways, that's replacing the intimacy you miss from when your mom did that. You're kind of trying to get back to that." Randy said. "My mother passed away when I was very little," he said. "So, some of my feelings from that have a great impact on my ability to form relationships with women. I'm probably making a pity party that my mother passed away when I was very young, but I feel like I've got, sort of, attachment and abandonment issues."

Mark went deeper into it. "One of the reasons why I became like this is because of my relationship with my mother," he said. "That's the first relationship that boys have, and when you're little, it can feel like a romantic relationship. You love her like that. I used to be a really affectionate little kid. I used to hug my mom and kiss my mom every time I saw her. She was everything to me.

"Then I turned thirteen, and I went to hug her, and she stuck her arm out and said, 'No. You ain't no baby no more. You can't be kissing and hugging on me no more. It's time for you to be a man.' I was like, 'What? Being a man means I can't hug and kiss you? That's only for little kids?' I didn't understand, and it felt kinda harsh to me. I felt like I had to be distant from her. Like, I couldn't show her how I felt. I think that relationship set the course for why I became a cheater. I was looking to get back to that closeness, and I wanted to get back at her for rejecting me. After that I didn't feel safe around women because I felt like eventually she's going to say no and hurt me. I think a lot of men won't admit it, but they go through the same thing."

A lot of men may not be cheating because they lacked something in their relationship with their mother, but a vast number of men suffer from a tremendous amount of inner turmoil that they don't talk about and that no one is aware of. Mark continued: "A lot of men walk around in a lot of pain, you know, and pain causes you to not be vulnerable. In order to love, you have to be vulnerable, and when you're hurt and you don't trust people, it's hard to be vulnerable and truly love, you know what I'm saying? So we replace love with sex."

Harry said, "A lot of men have what I call kicked puppy syndrome. You ever see a puppy that was abused so much that when you go to pet it, it flinches, or it balls up, or it growls at you because it's used to being mistreated? That's what's going on with a lot of men. I was one of those people who was mistreated, and I recoiled from people being nice to me. Then *I* became someone who mistreated people. I became a cheater because I didn't like myself."

Jill, a Revenge Cheater, said,

"I was completely devastated by my husband's cheating. Finding out that after six years of marriage he was having an affair with somebody else was like a cut to the throat. I really felt like a profound failure. And it made me so angry. It left me with a lot of regret and anger at myself, even more so than at him." She doesn't deserve that. If a guy is on a sports team, and he screws up and costs his team a game, afterward in the locker room he'll stand up and say, "That was my fault." To refuse to accept guilt or to instead point fingers at other players would be unthinkable. Well, marriage is a team for life, and after a man gets caught cheating, a stand-up guy will admit it, accept blame, and be open to answering her questions.

Being honest is honorable and prevents the deceived wife from being further traumatized. Of course, it does not always save the marriage. For many couples, the moment that an affair comes to light is extremely painful and traumatic, but as surprising as this might be to believe, for many couples, it's like a blessing in disguise. Once the dust settles, they have a make-or-break moment. There's a chance to begin saving and rebuilding their relationship. There's a chance to reset. People can be honest and admit the problems that led them to this place and see if they can salvage this and make life better for both. In so many cases, the revelation of an affair is not the end of the relationship but the beginning of a new chapter. After an affair is discovered, a couple can propel themselves into a much-needed conversation about who each of them really is, what they really need from each other, and why one of them felt like he or she needed to go outside the marriage for sexual and emotional fulfillment. If a couple can grapple with what's really going on between them, if they can have that radical honesty, it can help them get past whatever is separating them and pull them closer together and create a better relationship.

For men, talking on a deep level about themselves and their emotions is hard. Men are forced to deal with mountains of societal conditioning that discourages them from becoming emotionally aware or to value their own feelings enough to share them. Instead, they're taught to avoid complaining and to submerge their pain rather than confront it—whether that's by drinking, doing drugs, working out obsessively, or watching porn. It's not his wife's fault that he didn't share, but when it comes time for a Big Talk, if she wants to salvage the relationship, she may need to be really intentional about creating a safe space for him to share his feelings with her. Yes, she may be incredibly angry and hurt, but if a man cheated because he was afraid or unable to share his deepest feelings with her, or if he was not able to value his feelings enough to do the work of sharing them with her, then she may need to help set up a stage on which he can share his heart. That just means that if she wants to hear his whys, she may have to help him find a way to share them. Even if she wants to leave him, she can make it easier for him to share his heart and his motivations, and if she does, it will make it easier for her to walk away without feeling responsible for ending the marriage. Even if she doesn't blame herself, it will be easier for her to understand what really happened.

She may wonder, "Why should I do anything to help this cheater?" That's understandable. But she should know that society has long told him that his feelings don't matter, and that may be part of why he cheated. Unlike her, he's got a lot of social coding to overcome just to be able to share. She's been told since she was young that she should be in touch with her feelings and share them. At this critical juncture in his life, he must ignore the voices that say men shouldn't be in touch with their feelings, because this is the time that a clear and honest understanding of his feelings could save his family. If a man can truly share himself honestly and if his wife can truly hear him.

Several cheaters told me they were totally willing to cry in order to save their marriage if caught cheating, but are those just performative tears to evoke her sympathy or an expression of the real pain inside him? If saving his marriage is truly an imperative, he should dig deeper than just tears.

Harry said, "I think our inability to really sit down and bring the issues to the table and work with our spouses is because men aren't allowed a wide range of emotional outlets. We're expected to have a small range of feelings. Like, we feel the same emotions, but how are we supposed to express them? We're not." Several men said that their gender's inability or unwillingness to explore and discuss their deepest feelings is why they cheat. As complicated as philandering is, for many men it's still easier than talking. It fulfills so much of what men are taught to do: don't complain, take care of yourself, solve your own problems. In many cases, men say they went into an affair to avoid dealing with problems at home.

Ray from Boston said, "I feel like a lot of men will give up when things get hard in their marriage. Instead of digging deep and trying to figure it out, they'll run away and have an affair and not deal. Hey, sometimes you're in love, and things are just not working. And if it's not working, guys will try to find other ways to make themselves happy, by stepping out and redirecting their energies. But the only thing you can really do is to work it out with your woman. Look, it takes a certain amount of determination and fortitude to stick with it. What I've found over the years as we ride this roller coaster of marriage is that there are highs and lows, but if you make it through the lows, the next high is going to

be higher. But you can't get there unless you're committed."
Once the affair is known, the cheater has got to do that work.
He owes his wife that much.

For most people, knowing what you really feel requires
talking through your emotions with another person. A
lot emerges from and gets clarified through verbalizing
thoughts and hearing them out loud and hearing another
mind process and reflect them back to you. In conversation
with someone who cares about you, you can come to realiza-
tions, make connections, and discover deeper truths. You can
also feel heard and seen. That in itself can make people feel
better and help them find the strength to take the concrete
steps they need to move toward a better approach to life.

If a cheater can resolve to think deeply about himself and
talk openly about who he is and why he's cheating and what
he needs, then he is taking a big step toward becoming a
better husband. Some men said their cheating had stemmed
from not knowing themselves well enough when they got
married. Their sense of self changed during their marriage,
which led to supplementing their needs by finding a girlfriend.

Larry from Chicago said, "As a younger individual, in my
opinion, you still have a lot to learn about yourself. In a relationship, you tend to find what it is you need after you understand yourself better. When you understand your whole self,
you can go after what you need to make you happy. I entered
my marriage in good faith, and I really believe that my in-

tentions were good, but there's something to the whole idea of finding yourself after seven or eight or nine years, and at that point, you may find you need something that your wife doesn't want to give. If that happens, it becomes very challenging to not be attracted to other people who might give you what you need. I think if anyone is honest with themselves, over the course of forty-five years of life, you've reinvented yourself at least three, four, or five times, with new goals and desires and things you'd never thought you'd be into." If a cheater has strayed because he wanted things his wife could not or would not provide, he should consider sharing with her how his needs have shifted, so that she can understand that his cheating was not a rejection of her, it was a reaction to himself and his desires.

Cheaters can possibly help figure out who they are by placing themselves into one of the five categories of cheaters. This could help them identify their deeper motivation. A cheater who recognizes the pattern of a Dead Bedroomer may find that he felt ignored and tossed aside at home. Perhaps the affair was an attempt to feel seen and appreciated. The cheater may want to ask for more attention and intimacy. After an affair, the couple need to talk their way through to a new understanding of what their marriage will be like.

A cheater who sees himself as a Peacock may realize that he needed an outsized amount of affirmation and reinforcement of his looks and his sexiness. He may not be able to have all his desires met in a single relationship, but he may need to ask himself why he needs to have so many people reconfirming his sexual attractiveness. What is he trying to prove? Why does he keep questioning it? He may want to explore why he needs that so badly that he's willing to put his life and his wife's happiness at risk. Is there a way of bottling the affirmation he's gotten in the past? Is there a way of building his self-confidence or addressing his insecurity so that he doesn't need constant reassurance? Is there a chance of minimizing the attention he needs from strangers? Is there a possibility of his wife fulfilling more of what he needs?

If the husband is a Completer, what is it about the thing that bonds the cheater to his affair partner that feels so necessary? Can that interest be fulfilled without seeking extramarital sex? Can he deepen his connection to his wife instead of to someone else? What is it about his past self that he needs to return to?

If he's a Revenge Cheater, both partners have work to do to explore why they cheated. They both have to work through their rage and see if there's still a viable relationship on the other side of those painful feelings. After the Revenge Cheater has exacted his or her payback, can the couple put that chapter behind them and reestablish trust?

If a cheater is an Emotional Connector, can he explore which feelings or connections he was getting from his other relationship? Above all, an affair is certainly painful, but it does not have to bring about the end of a marriage. If a cheater can be open and honest, if he can be self-reflective, if he can talk his way through to new understandings, if he can make a pledge to his wife and start to rebuild trust, if he can accept her anger and hurt, and truly and actively choose her, then what Jill called "the clock of healing" can begin, and the marriage can possibly survive and even grow stronger than it was before.

The cheater will have to accept that his partner has just learned about something that likely has been going on in his life for months or years. It will take time for her to process and come to grips with this information and the feelings that arise. She will certainly be traumatized by this revelation, and even if she forgives her husband, the probability of repeated traumatization is high—perhaps inevitable. This must be accepted as part of the healing process. As Ryan said, the issues resurface from time to time. Most men know that women tend to never forget things that have hurt them in a relationship. But cheaters should not fear the issue recurring in the future because coming clean means you have a chance to finally be heard, and that means a chance for the relationship to grow.

Larry said, "It's a shock to the system when you tell her what you did, and it's hard, but I think that people don't always want to leave you. And in that moment, you can rediscover each other, and you can maybe discover something that you never saw in each other. I'd say my wife had a very idealized sense of me, but after all this, she started to see me as more human, and it probably helped to have her get a better understanding of me, you know? I don't know really how to describe it, but I think she really saw me better afterward. It caused all kinds of other problems that are still ongoing, but even if we don't make it, I think that she's more in tune to who I am authentically than she was before, and she knows what I need from the relationship, and we're now worked on what we both want."

Many men spoke about not feeling seen before they were caught. Larry said, "Sometimes when you're not an active participant in a relationship, you feel like the days are just kinda droning on and on, and habit takes over. The kids go to practice and then ACT prep or whatever, and you're just vessels for things to happen, and the identity is lost. Both people are working toward goals, but they're not doing anything that cultivates or invests in the other person, and you don't feel loved. You feel like a ghost going through the motions. I think a lot of relationships I see get to be like that.

"I think it's better to have a relationship that's more vulnerable, where you can be present, instead of just waking up and having it happen to you. For me, when we fell into that rut, I went out and did my thing, and when she found out, and everything went haywire, that's when we were able to talk in a real way and eventually get back to being able to really see each other."

Guys who reject humility, who refuse to do the emotional work necessary to put proper context and closure on the marriage, are leaving their wives with a mess to clean up. They may also be launching themselves into an empty future. One person who found that out the hard way is Lucas whose marriage crumbled after his affairs were revealed.

"I had rules with my girlfriends," said Lucas, a total Peacock. "I had time frames and stuff that I wouldn't bend because I knew it would look shady to my wife. But then I started bending my rules to one chick's availability because she had a husband. She started getting into this whole thing of, like, 'Come over at midnight.' At first, I was, like, 'Oh, I can't do that,' but I also felt like I really wanted to hit that again. So, I started bending my rules. Next thing you know, I'm coming home at three in the morning because I felt like I had a right to do whatever I wanted.

But then I started really liking the wildness of it all, and I started getting to a point where I thought I wanted to be single again. So I kind of *let* myself get caught. I think I was in a moment of self-destruction, and I wanted to be single—like, I didn't want to divorce her, but if she initiated it, then it's on her, and then I could go back to living the wild single life. So I just admitted to it. I could have denied it and slithered away, but I was, like, 'Yeah, I did it; now what?'

"So I got kicked out. I went and got myself one of those super fly apartments downtown, and I went ahead and lived that life. I was fucking chicks left and right and dating and doing all that, and I was living the dream. This is what I thought it would be like. But after running through several girls, I was thinking, *What is this? Where is this going?* I was, like, *This isn't what I want. I need more.*

"I tried getting into prostitutes, but I found that I can't hand over money and fuck and leave. I needed more. So, I went into the red-light distinct in Amsterdam, the Netherlands, and I found this chick who was bad as hell. I went into her room and gave her the money, and my dick would not get hard. I tried and tried, but it just would not play along, no matter what I did. She was, like, 'You're in the wrong place. You need love and conversation. This isn't the place for that.' She ripped the condom right off and threw me out. I was like, *Damn!*"

An affair is rarely going to lead to a stable, fulfilling relationship—none of the people I interviewed who left his marriage for his affair partner ended up happy. Part of what supercharges the affair is the secrecy and the wrongness of it all. When you subtract the drama from most affairs, the relationship has very little left to bond over.

Committing adultery is evidence that something is missing from a marriage, but it also drives the couple into more problems because it diverts a man's mind and his energy and his emotions into another relationship and causes him to lead a secret life that he's not sharing, which is antithetical to romantic closeness. An affair can be like a malignant tumor in the body of a relationship, eating away at its health. No one can truly multitask and reach maximum effectiveness—if you're multitasking, you're devoting only a part of yourself to each task, not all of yourself to any one of them. If you're in two relationships, you're giving part of yourself to two women, and neither one is getting all of you. Men said that cheating helps them shove away the annoyance and the pain when their main relationship doesn't take care of them, but what that means is they have an outlet but are avoiding the actual issues. They're not pouring themselves into their marriage in a way that will lead to them sharing and confronting issues and being a full partner.

Sam from New Orleans said, "When stuff happens at home, you shake it off, and you think, *Screw it, I have a whole other girlfriend, so be as crazy as you want to be.* So, you start to lose some empathy for your wife. I became pretty robotic in terms of feeling because I didn't care. 'You're mad at me? Sure, okay, I'll do better'—but with no real feeling. Whenever my wife hurt me, I just shut down because I knew my girlfriend would make me happy." But a girlfriend is just a Band-Aid. If the man doesn't address the wound in his marriage, then eventually he's going to develop much bigger problems.

Many people said being seen, being open, being honest, and shedding the stress that comes with cheating can lead a man to a deep level of peace. "After I got caught, I felt good," said Eddie the engineer. "I felt relieved 'cause I didn't have to lie. Everything is out in the open. That was a relief when I could just do things without having to remember everything and compartmentalize everything and rehearse lies so that I didn't slip up. I could just *live*. When you're fooling around, there's a lot of steps that you have to take to cover your tracks. You're constantly on high alert with your electronics and your socials, and you have to worry about where you're going and where your wife might be and where everyone who knows her might be. I would always be on guard, which is stressful.

"But once she found out, I was okay. I didn't have to hide anymore. I can step out in the open. Life is not as stressful as it was before she found out. I always wanted to enjoy a relationship that was stress free, where neither of us was cheating. We're both into each other, and we enjoy each other. We look out for each other, and I have that now. Whereas before, my wife thought that because we were married, she didn't have to work at the marriage. Now we both know that we do."

Kevin said that after his wife caught him, he had an epiphany. "I was, like, *Holy shit! Why would I want to hurt this person? I mean, I love this person!* I have fun with them, we have a great time, and she takes care of me and looks out for my emotional well-being. Why would I put her emotional well-being into jeopardy? And in that instant, I realized how detrimental cheating is, and I said to myself, *I'm never cheating again.* And that was the end of that."

One of the most extraordinary stories from my research came from a man who called me three days after our interview to say that our conversation had weighed heavily on him in the days after we spoke and the sound of his own stories had ricocheted through his head until it was too much.

"I was harboring so much stuff that I did behind my wife's back," he said, "and I felt a lot of guilt. And I ended up pretty much confessing everything to her. I told her I'd had sex with all of these women. I told her how many women I had sex with and everything. It pretty much just allowed me to just get a whole bunch of stuff off my chest that I needed to get off. I just realized that I couldn't put these stories out there if she didn't know.

"She respected the fact that I told her. She said it kinda allowed her to understand some things that she didn't really have any answers to. And it felt good to me as a man to tell her because it made me realize that I am changing as a man. If you want to be in a nice, stable relationship where you're building a future, you can't be out there running around with all these women."